OVERTIME

A Football Coach's Journey from Wounded Child to Becoming a Man

BEN JACOBS

WestBow
PRESS
A DIVISION OF THOMAS NELSON

This story is based on true events. Some of the names of characters have been changed

WestBow Press books may be ordered through booksellers or by contacting:

WestBow Press
A Division of Thomas Nelson
1663 Liberty Drive
Bloomington, IN 47403
www.westbowpress.com
1-(866) 928-1240

ISBN: 978-1-4497-3267-7 (hc)
ISBN: 978-1-4497-3266-0 (sc)
ISBN: 978-1-4497-3265-3 (e)
Library of Congress Control Number: 2011961172

Printed in the United States of America

WestBow Press rev. date: 12/21/2011

TO MY GIRLS

To Mandy, Isabella, and Ava, for their love and humor.
I love you girls. Y'all are always on my mind.

ACKNOWLEDGMENTS

I'm a little bit embarrassed by how easily my psyche can be bruised. I'm also slightly ashamed by my minor and brief brushes with the law. But, I think it was a necessary path that I had to take. After all, it was all part of God's plan for me.

I'm eternally grateful to Neal LaHue for the Christmas present that he gave me. Intentionally, or unintentionally, he gave me the gift of inspiration.

I also find it necessary to thank Jeffrey Marx and Joe Ehrmann. Without their life stories, my book could not have been written.

The writing of this book required that I get to know my football players in a whole different way. I'd like to thank a few of them for sharing their lives with me: Joshua Glass, Sean Alonzo, Christian Pastrano, Elias Rodriguez and Leland Young.

I must also thank my wife Mandy Jacobs. Without her expertise in computer software, I could not have finished this project. I also want to thank her for never judging me about some of the poor choices that I have made along my journey to becoming a man.

I also need to thank my mother and father for their willingness to share with me. I know it was not easy talking about the past, and I know that it was a little painful. Again, thank you.

I need to thank the many great men that I have coached with at Austin, Reagan, Travis and Roosevelt high schools: Mickey Moss, David Hoff, Tom Mueller, Glenn Bacak, Steve Ramsey, Roosevelt Nivens, Tim

Warfield, J.L. Geist, Paul Waldon, Billy Brown, Todd Patmon, Richard Reyes, Mickey Bushong, Harry Brooks, Ken Bush, Joe Frank Martinez, David Harsh, Glen Lewis, Calvin Ivey, Glenn Hill, Jeff Hooks, Joe Matulich, Matt Carroll, John Williams, Richard Severyns, Brad Robinson, Lee Miller, William Lynch, Clay Johnson, Kevin Palmer, Brett Griffin, Lyndon Hamilton, Ben Cook, Tate DeMasco, Patrick Swoyer, Anthony Boykin and Gene Scoggins.

"A heart is not judged by how much you love, but by how much you are loved by others."

WIZARD OF OZ, 1939

Chapter 1

Twelve seconds remained on the scoreboard. It was a beautiful October night, and the backdrop to Heroes Stadium was magnificent, hugging the edge of a cliff. The stadium had been built in a large quarry. The cavernous, brand new stadium overlooked a busy Interstate-35.

My Theodore Roosevelt Rough Riders held a 28-21 lead over the MacArthur Brahmas, the top-ranked team in San Antonio. The 4,426 fans at Heroes Stadium sat on the edge of their seats. For the past forty-seven minutes and forty-eight seconds, they had witnessed an epic battle.

The Rough Riders sported white jerseys and navy pants. Our solid white helmets and white face masks glistened under the stadium lights, giving us a storm trooper look. Only the helmet's decal, a red *TR* outlined in navy, seemed not to be reflecting the massive stadium lights.

From the stands, it may have appeared that all was calm on our sideline, but the pulse of our players and coaching staff was running high to say the least. It was hard not to stare at the scoreboard, as if somehow the remaining time would expire faster. Nervous young men paced back and forth.

As a high school football coach and fan of the game, I realized this great game was coming to an end. It was fourth and long for the Brahmas from our thirty-one yard line. The Brahmas were out of time outs. A field goal would do them absolutely no good. They had to score a touchdown.

We knew they were going to have to throw the football, and we knew who they were going to throw it to. MacArthur possessed one of the best players in the state of Texas in tight end/wide receiver Jace Amarro. Texas Tech University thought so highly of him that they had offered him a full scholarship before his senior season began.

My corner backs played softer than our usual alignment, paying special attention to the clock and knowing that a deep vertical pass was coming their way. We were ready. We back pedaled; we were in good position, and the football was thrown high into the warm, black night. It fell harmlessly to the ground.

That was the ball game, we had won! But as we celebrated on the field and our offense huddled on the sideline to prepare to take a knee, the sideline official informed us that there was a penalty flag lying on the turf: pass interference on the Rough Riders.

Pass interference is a penalty that occurs when a player interferes with a receiver's ability to make an attempt to catch a pass. We couldn't believe it; if anything, we felt Amarro had interfered with the defender who was in a great position to intercept the football.

I stared out at the green field turf where the bright yellow penalty flag was thrown. Most spectators just see Astro-turf or grass when they look out at a stadium's playing surface. But not me; I saw something else entirely, a cathedral. And at that moment, I feared that perhaps the Lord was punishing me for some of my wild excursions as a college student or sins that I had committed as an adult.

MacArthur was given the ball at our sixteen yard line and a new set of downs. There was just enough clock left that we knew they were going to throw the jump ball fade to Amarro. We had performed this exact scenario in practice. We had a bracket called, which meant that the weak side corner was to bang the wide receiver and funnel him inside, allowing the free safety to play high and over the top of the play. Four seconds remained; this was going to be the last play of the game.

The corner banged Amarro at the line of scrimmage, and our free safety, Leland Young played it perfectly. He was high and over the top of the play. He high pointed the ball and intercepted it. As he sprinted with the ball, Young had noticed that time had expired, and he fell to the ground. We ran onto the field and celebrated once again, jumping for joy. Hugs were abundant, cherishing the fact that this time it counted. We had just won a game that no one other than our own coaches and players thought we could win.

The officials were trying to get us back to our sideline. I clearly remember thinking that we just got flagged for excessive celebration, but at that point, who cared? We were going to have some fun.

Apparently, the back judge had thrown a late penalty flag and decided that we interfered with Amarro again. Later in the evening, after watching the play many times on video, I still couldn't really see what the official felt that he saw. Nevertheless, the call stood.

The official marked the ball at the one yard line. MacArthur was to be given one untimed down. Shell-shocked, we called time out to regroup.

Two plays earlier, the game's outcome seemed certain. We had already overcome so much adversity (on and off the field) that this just didn't seem possible.

Sweat-filled jerseys stuck to the players' bodies, and the young men tried to calm their breathing as we talked to them. Large, green, trademarked Gatorade water bottles were passed around and gulped down in a hurry. Our players were exhausted, physically and mentally.

We jogged back onto the field and waited for the official to blow his whistle, letting everyone know that the play could be run.

The football was snapped and MacArthur executed a perfectly thrown fade route into the corner of the end zone. Touchdown Brahmas.

Overtime.

As the MacArthur band trumpeted away, another sound blended in with the noise. Our fans were booing loudly, and shouting obscenities at the officials. I thought, *this can't be happening.*

Chapter 2

I stood in my bathroom staring at myself in the huge glass mirror that hung above the sink. I momentarily looked away from the mirror and touched the smooth, white, cultured-marble counter-top with my hands. I was looking for something.

It had been a rather brisk December evening, but it was warm inside my house, and from where I stood, the vent was pumping much wanted warm air over my body.

Looking at myself in the mirror during the 2010 Christmas holidays, I had come to the conclusion that I didn't necessarily like what I saw.

At first glance I saw an aging thirty-six year old man. My jet black hair was thinning, and peppered with streaks of grey and silver. My dark brown eyes stared back at me, while my black pupils continued to dilate as I studied myself. Light brown freckles penetrated my tan face.

Did I have a purpose in this world? Why was I here? Surely it was not just to win high school football games. *What kind of man was I?*

I thought about that for a while as I continued to stand in the bathroom. *Did I help others? Did I make others lives better?*

After much thought, I made some assumptions: I was a good father but a very average husband. I was an above average teacher who really became an educator because of my passion to help children. I felt like I was a great high school football coach who recently had been hardened as a man because of where I coached, and I was afraid.

I was afraid that, up to this point, I had lived life for all the wrong reasons, and that I had misguided values. I also felt like I had not made a big enough impact on some of the kids that I had coached. I was going to make some changes, I had to. *But how?*

It had been a tough year. My grandfather Sandy had died;Mark, a very close friend of mine, had recently passed away; and several great young men I had coached would soon be graduating. I never really expressed to any of them just how much I loved them.

My life truly changed, and, in many ways, started on the morning of January 4, 2011. I was thirty-six years old.

I felt it was time to try to teach young men about life, and that winning isn't always about putting more points on the scoreboard than your opponent. I wanted to make a difference in the world. I wanted the boys I coached to become special men. I felt that somehow I needed to do more. I targeted a group of young men that I thought either possessed leadership qualities or that needed a positive influence in their lives.

I invited eighteen football players. They had only been told that we were going to have a meeting in the morning and that I wanted them to attend. The meeting was to take place in the Roosevelt team room. The team room is a spacious room where we often met as a team, to either stretch, or watch film. It was large enough to comfortably sit about a hundred players.

"What are we going to meet and talk about?" outside linebacker Elias Rodriguez asked.

"Life," I said. "I'm going to talk to y'all about being a man, and learning how to love and be loved."

"Love? What about football, Coach? I want to get better," Elias said.

"What about football?" I said. "Football has nothing to do with what we'll be talking about. We'll be talking about what being a man truly is. Whether you are a good or bad football player doesn't have anything to do with being a good man."

"But Coach, I want to win. I want to go to the playoffs," Elias said.

"I don't care if we don't win a single game," I said. "I want us to win in the game of life." I could see Elias was confused and his head was swimming, as he looked somewhat stunned. "Oh, okay, Coach," Elias said. "I'll see you tomorrow."

I had no doubt that he would show up. I had sunk an anchor into him and he wanted to know what in the world I was talking about.

At eight o'clock, on a cold and dark Tuesday morning, our first ever Turning Boyz into Men meeting began. Sixteen players showed up. They were on time. I was shocked; I didn't know if anybody other than Elias would actually show up. They quickly grabbed a seat and looked up at the power point presentation that was on screen courtesy of the projector. There was a question displayed.

What makes a Man a Man?

That was my question that I asked them. The power point slide stared at them on a pull down screen often used for viewing and evaluating football film.

I looked at the young men, as they looked back at me with wide-eyed stares, wanting to be taught and eager to learn.

Over the next thirty minutes we discussed many things, mainly what it means to be a man. While teaching, perhaps even preaching, I enjoyed the sounds and sights of young men discussing life, and thinking about their futures.

Later in the day, Joshua Glass, our second team all-district strong safety came and found me in the hall way. He was glowing.

"Coach, it was great. There will be more kids next meeting," Joshua said. "Wait until I talk to them about it."

He was right, twenty-one to be exact.

Chapter 3

Roosevelt High School sits in one of the poorest zip codes in San Antonio. Roosevelt, or the "Velt," as it is affectionately called by our student athletes, is geographically located on 5110 Walzem Road, in the North East part of San Antonio.

Pawn shops and 'quick' loan stores are lined up and down Walzem Road. A closed Target and failed shopping mall are quick visual reminders that the area has fallen upon hard times. The Target closed just weeks after my hire date at Roosevelt in July of 2005. Windsor Park Mall had been closed for several years prior to my arrival.

Windsor Park Mall was arguably once the mall to go shopping at in San Antonio. But now, just over one million square feet sat barren and vacated.

Loitering, theft, and violence were just a few of the reasons the businesses had failed to thrive.

Roosevelt had once been an all white high school made up of working class families in the mid-1970's.

It was now all African-American and Hispanic, with a handful of white and Asian students; consisting of mostly low socio-economic families. Eighty-six percent of our student body was on free or reduced lunch.

Needless to say, lack of transportation is an obstacle that the Roosevelt community faces. From time to time it is not uncommon for a coach to drive an athlete home. For many of our football players it becomes a part of their daily routine. "Coach, I'm ready, can you take me home?"

Directly across the street from our football field is a set of run down apartments. I thought that a quarterback with a strong arm could probably hit the apartments with a good throw.

The apartment complex is a well known home to drug dealers, drug users, and other criminal activities. Police and ambulance sirens can often be heard entering and leaving as we conduct drills during football practice.

Just minutes after we left the practice field on a scorching hot Spring day, gun shots rang out. "Somebody just got smoked," said one of our football players.

We were still in school. The sound of a nearby helicopter was easily recognized as we entered our dressing room.

Within minutes an announcement was made over the school's P.A. system.

"Teachers. Please do not release students until you are told to do so. Thank you."

"Oh man," said a disappointed football player.

Almost seconds later another announcement was made.

"Teachers, please lock your door and do not release any student to go home. You will receive more instructions shortly. I repeat, please keep all students in your class room."

We didn't know it yet, but apparently two people had been murdered not far from where we just had practiced. It had happened just moments before the bell was to ring to release students for the day.

The entire school was 'locked down' as we had to hold the students in our rooms. In my case, the locker room. All 2,856 Roosevelt students waited an additional thirty-two minutes after the school day had ended until the North East ISD Police department deemed it safe enough to release students.

I stood and stared at one of the walls that led to the ninth grade boys' locker room. Sweat and sour clothes combined to make a wretched odor. I wrinkled my nose as I continued to stare at the wall while the boys changed into their outfits they had worn to school. On the wall was one of many flyers I had stuck anywhere that I thought a football player might look at.

> *Coming this fall*
> *MAKING MEN*
> *Character Education*
> *We will meet every*
> *Thursday*

My thoughts drifted off and I had a flashback to my third year at Roosevelt. A promising defensive back I had coached was gunned down, shot twice at close range, and murdered. The back of his head had been blown out, and apparently his body lay in a bloody pool in the middle of his neighborhood street. He was only fifteen years old.

I was tired of the violence that seemed to plague our east side high school. I thought to myself, *it may never end.*

It was only April. It was going to be a long spring.

The 2011 school year seemed to be stuck on the rewind button, and I needed it to play out. Summer felt far, far away.

Chapter 4

The nomadic existence I had come to know as a high school football coach would continue with the conclusion of the 2004 season. The roller coaster ride of events and circumstances that indirectly brought me to San Antonio Roosevelt of North East ISD began when Coach Wayne Williams gave me a demotion after I helped lead his Austin Travis Rebels to a 7-4 bi-district playoff appearance.

I was pissed! I couldn't believe it, I felt like I had been stabbed in the back. I had left my job as defensive coordinator at Austin Reagan to help my friend turn a perennial loser into a winner, virtually overnight.

During my two year stint as defensive coordinator with the Reagan Raiders we had gone 16-8, playing in four playoff games. Now I was basically being told that I would be a sub-varsity coach. My ego and my feelings were bruised.

I had first met Coach Williams in the spring of 2001. Austin High School head football Coach Mickey Moss had hired Wayne as an assistant after Sam Houston High School had let him go after twenty-four seasons.

Wayne was a thin fifty something year old white male. He was still an avid jogger and a charming man to be around. He had the uncanny ability to make you feel safe. Football was an important part of his life, and we would have never met if we did not share the same passion: winning high school football games. He was also Godfather to one of my best friends.

We were introduced to each other while I was folding jock straps in the equipment room. The equipment room was a tiny—hot stuffy room that housed all of our shoulder pads, helmets, and any other piece of equipment that was needed to outfit a football team.

I was in charge of football equipment my last season at Austin High and I took a lot of pride in it. Wayne was supposed to help me with the spring inventory. Wayne eye balled me and then looked at the hundreds of T-shirts and shorts that still needed to be folded. I could tell in an instant he did not want any part of this assignment.

"Don't worry about it (helping me), I got it." I said.

"Thanks Coach," Wayne said.

"No problem," I said as I continued to fold the jock straps.

Wayne remembered that and hired me as co-offensive coordinator at Austin Travis in the spring of 2004.

Wayne was actually only at Austin High less than a few weeks before he was named head coach at south Austin's William B. Travis High School. He immediately offered me a job. I declined the offer but we would be re-united three years later.

Unfortunately, my time at Travis was short lived and very frustrating.

It didn't take long at all before I dreaded our staff meetings. Staff meetings are when the entire football coaching staff would come together, often under the direction of our head coach. Once there, we would discuss schemes, and personnel or practice schedules. After just a few staff meetings it was crystal clear to me that there was not much purpose in us meeting.

Wayne was too much of a nice guy, and very Wayne was too much of a nice guy, and very flaky. Whoever went into his office last was the idea or scheme we were going to go with. I couldn't coordinate that way.

Ultimately, I finished up with official titles of special teams coordinator and head secondary coach.

Travis had been 1-9, 0-9-1, and 1-9 prior to my arrival. There is no nice way to put it; Travis had been awful! They weren't just losing; they were getting blown out almost every week. The challenge ahead of me enticed me, I knew that I could coach, but we would have to change the players whole mind set. It's hard to win when you have never won; I was going to coach hard, by any means necessary. It worked, and it didn't.

Motivating the players was easy; they were hungry and wanted to win. They did just about everything that was asked of them.

Because I had coached against Travis the past four seasons and we had won by scores of 48-0, 66-6, 47-0, and 47-14, I just honestly didn't think much of the present coaching staff. I know that's terribly arrogant, but at that time in my life that's how I thought. Unintentionally, I think I alienated a few members of the coaching staff.

I think from a football standpoint everyone was excited to have me on board, and on the football field most of my ideas worked. We were explosive on special teams, and our opponents eventually stopped kicking to us.

If I was going to be in charge of running the special teams, we were going to be damn good at it. Coach Glen Lewis, David Harsh, Joe Frank Martinez, and Calvin Ivey assisted me with the special teams. They did a great job of teaching their assignments. We ran the starburst on kickoff returns. The starburst is a kickoff return that through a series of fakes and possible handoffs could have as many as four possible ball carriers.

We also ran a wall reverse on punt returns, and we were not afraid to onside kick in the middle of a game or fake a punt. An onside kick is an intentionally short kickoff that travels forward the required ten yards, which the kicking team can attempt to recover. We put pressure on our opponents.

Our home field was Burger Center, located in South Austin right off of Highway 71. I had fond memories of having played there when I was a wide receiver at Austin High School.

During my senior year at Austin High school I had caught four passes for fifty yards against the Travis Rebels at this very field. Now I was coaching on it; the very same grass and field I had watched the Dallas Cowboys scrimmage on during training camp. I smiled as our yellow bus parked on the west side of the stadium.

It was our season opener, and I believed this game to be huge for us.

The smell of the diesel engine filled my nostrils as I walked off the bus and into our dressing room.

After the kids had dropped off their pads and sat down for some quiet time, I escaped for a few minutes down the hall. There was a restroom for officials and coaches away from the players' dressing room, and I was thankful for it. I wanted to be alone for a few minutes. My stomach was a bundle of knots; nerves were getting the best of me. I took my pre-game shit, and then soaked my head under the faucet in the sink. The cold water felt good as it saturated my scalp.

I was nervous! I was hoping I was as good as I thought I was, I was hoping our team played well, I was hoping we would win. I hoped.

In what would become kind of a tradition, at least for one season, and certainly part of our pregame preparation, I wrote a phrase on the chalk board that would be written at least ten more times.

"Winning . . . think how good it's going to feel."

I believe psychology can be used in sports, and I was going to test my theory.

We needed a win to start the 2004 season rolling in the right direction.

Was I nuts for taking this job? Travis had only won two games over the past three seasons. I felt that we had to win this game; we had to open the season with a win. Losing can be like a disease, and when you've been losing, you come to expect it. It's easy to keep losing, or so I thought.

We won our season opener with a thrilling 27-21 win over Austin Akins. We had to make a goal line stand on the game's final play to preserve the win. When the game ended I looked to find Wayne. I wanted to shake his hand (I was not a hugger yet with other men) and tell him congratulations. He could not be found.

He later told me that he had jogged to the locker room because he was crying; he couldn't believe that we had won and was overcome with emotion. I celebrated with the players, it was a great moment. The kids played hard, and we often forget as coaches that the kids are the ones who have to go out and play, execute and ultimately win or lose. The win was even sweeter for me because midway through the first quarter both of my starting safeties were ejected for exchanging punches with the other team.

Backup strong safety Jose Ramon intercepted a pass and returned it for the game winning touchdown. Jose was a great kid, not the most talented player, as he would fully admit, and it was really fun watching him lumber in for the score.

Week two would reunite with me two former Reagan Raiders and friends. Both Coach Mickey Bushong and Coach Mike Christensen were now coaching at Hutto. It's a strange feeling to have to coach against your friends. Hutto was very talented, and they had just blown out their first opponent by sixty-four points the week before.

Hutto High sported one of my all time favorite mascot names. The Hippos were led by quarterback Jeremy Kerley. Kerley was an incredible player. He would later play a huge role on the Texas Christian University team that finished 13-0 in 2010, defeating Wisconsin in the Rose Bowl. On September 11, 2011, Kerley returned punts for the New York Jets on opening day versus the Dallas Cowboys.

We played well early, and led Hutto 13-0 at the half. But it was short lived, Hutto stormed out of the gates and defeated us 34-18. Walking across the field on a warm September evening, I exchanged handshakes with my friends, and congratulated the opposing team.

We had three days to prepare for San Antonio John F. Kennedy, our next opponent. Although you have a full week in between games, you really don't. Monday through Wednesday you put everything in (all of your scouting report) and attempt to simulate your opponent's offense and defense, as well as tweak your own schemes. Thursday is more or less a walk through day, (that you don't hit each other) and make sure that the right people run on and off the field as you call for your special teams. Each week presents a new challenge, and this week it was to beat JFK.

We drove down to San Antonio on the charter bus; the bus ride was air-conditioned and just long enough to catch a nap. Just about the whole trip we drove south on Interstate—35. I awoke as the kids oohed and aahed as we drove the past the Alamodome. The Alamodome is a huge multi-purpose stadium that hosts college bowl games, and sometimes college basketball's *Final Four*. It was also once the home of the San Antonio Spurs as well as a temporary fix for the New Orleans Saints while the Superdome was being fixed due to Hurricane Katrina's wrath.

We had left school a little early that day so we could avoid getting caught in traffic. In addition, we wanted to walk the field and make it a fun day for our kids. A lot of our kids had never been outside of the Austin city limits before. We went to a city park near Mata Stadium and ate with the kids. The defensive backs and I found a table in the corner under a covered pavilion. I had wanted us to sit somewhere we would be shielded from the boiling Texas sun.

After eating our sacked lunches, the defensive backs and I discussed a few things I was concerned about defensively; I saw that I didn't really have their full attention. I stopped talking and just kind of enjoyed the sights and sounds with the kids. I guess if we didn't know our assignments by now, we were not going to know them.

The secondary played very well. The secondary consists of two cornerbacks and two safeties, often referred to as defensive backs. The secondary are players on the defensive side of the ball who cover receivers.

We intercepted two balls and nearly scored on one of the returns.

In the fading Friday light, the Travis Rebels executed the starburst to near perfection, returning the opening kickoff to our opponents forty-two yard line. After another long return they didn't kick it deep again. Soon it was night, and the last of the clear blue sky and puffy white clouds vanished.

It was a pretty sloppy 30-23 overtime victory for the Travis Rebels. But, after winning only two games the previous three years combined, the Travis Rebels were more than happy to be 2-1. We drove the kids down to the Alamo and let them walk around for awhile; it was a great night for all of us.

San Antonio Fox Tech was our fourth opponent. They would have to come to Burger Stadium, where we seemed to play well.

After watching their game films, I was convinced that we could recover a sneaky onside kick against them. Their whole left side left early and never ensured that the football was kicked deep. I was more than sure that we could do it.

I convinced Wayne it would work. We practiced it, over and over.

Early second quarter we scored to go up 21-7. I thought it was the perfect time for a sneaky onside kick. I went over and asked Wayne what he thought.

"Do it," Wayne said. It worked to perfection. There was not a Fox Tech player within ten yards when we fell on the kick. The Buffaloes were shocked; we took full advantage. With the quick change of possession we went for the knockout punch. The game was essentially over. We cruised to an easy 36-21 victory. The Rebels were now 3-1 and gaining confidence.

Marble Falls would be our fifth and final non-district opponent; we were well prepared and probably played our best game of the season. We scored on a ninety yard kickoff return early in the game and dominated all night.

Right before the end of the first half I witnessed something I had never seen before, and will probably never see again.

We scored a touchdown on a deep post, but it was called back because of a penalty: offensive holding was the call signaled by the official. Offensive holding is illegally blocking a player from the opposing team by grabbing and holding his uniform or body. We ran the exact same play and scored again. But wait, there was another penalty flag lying on the ground. Holding. There was only time for one more play, and we were now on about the fifty yard line. Everyone thought they knew where the ball was going, but our stud wide receiver, Daniel Brinkley, was tired, actually exhausted. After scoring on consecutive deep posts only to have them nullified, he was gassed. Our deep vertical threat was gone. I thought, *how on Earth are we going to score now?*

We decided to run a tailback screen. Tailback Kenny Williams gathered the ball in and managed to elude several defenders. He scampered into the end zone. There were no penalty flags on this play, this time the touchdown counted. Three scores on three consecutive plays. The route was officially on, final score: Rebels 48—Mustangs 21.

In our district opener, we opened with district favorite McCallum, who was decked out in blue jerseys and silver helmets. It made for an interesting show of color as we were wearing our road white jerseys and red pants.

The Knights had a good team, but I felt like we had a chance to beat them. The Knights were physically superior to us, and in terms of brute strength we were overmatched. I felt like our only option we had was to out scheme them. We didn't.

I had noticed some flaws in their special teams that I hoped we would exploit. We took an early 6-0 lead. After blocking our Point After Touchdown, McCallum received a fifteen yard penalty for unsportsmanlike conduct. We were going to kick off from their forty-five yard line.

I badly wanted to attempt an onside kick. The Knights did not have their hands team on the field and looked distraught and out of sync. A hands team is a group of players, often wide receivers, that are responsible for recovering an onside kick. Wide receivers are usually on most hands teams. They often have the best hands and are used to handling the football. Wayne wanted it kicked deep, so we kicked it out of the end zone.

I saw no disadvantage to attempting an onside kick. If we didn't recover it, the Knights would more than likely start their next possession on their own thirty yard line, leaving them seventy yards of ground they would have to cover to score a touchdown. I figured that ten yards of field position was well worth the risk. To this day, I wish we would have attempted the onside kick. I felt like the Knights would have folded up their tents and quit playing. I guess I'll never know.

Later in the half we did attempt and successfully execute a fake punt. But the Knights were too good, and went on to win by a final score of 43-18.

We were 0-1 in District play, but the good news was that we played the Johnston Rams next, and they were just not a very good football team.

We had our way with the Rams, and enjoyed a 42-6 victory.

Next up was Austin LBJ, a team with a lot of speed and athleticism. LBJ had some terrific teams in the 1980's and 1990's, but had failed to make the playoffs in each of the past two seasons. LBJ had once been home to some of the best tailbacks around: the Texas Longhorns' Shon Mitchel and the New England Patriots' Sedric Shaw are just a couple of names that always pop to the top of my head.

Regardless, I was very confident. Many members of the Travis coaching staff had voiced to me that our kids have been intimidated by LBJ in past matchups and they had not beaten the Jaguars in many years.

I was still not very worried. I should have been.

Warming up our guys on the side line with some pre-game popping of the pads, I heard—"Hey, Coach Jacobs, what's going on?"

I looked up and was temporarily blinded by Nelson Field's bright stadium lights.

It was Todd Patmon, my former boss at Reagan. He had gone down by our side to say hello and chat. It was a fun, fleeting moment. I missed Todd, and felt for him, Reagan was 1-7 and losing, and losing badly.

The LBJ-Travis game was crazy and totally unpredictable, and filled with many intense moments. At the end of regulation play, forty-eight official minutes later, the game was deadlocked.

Overtime.

LBJ received the ball first. On third and long one of my defensive backs, Eric Tennison, intercepted the ball in the end zone.

All we had to do was kick a field goal and the game would be over.

But, I guess it was not meant to be as our field goal attempt sailed wide left.

In double overtime we had the ball first and scored, the PAT was good.

The Jaguars had little problem scoring on their possession. But there would not be a third overtime.

The Jaguars lined up for the two point conversion and the win.

They decided to run a toss sweep.

Tennison had good leverage, and forced the tailback to cut back inside; our line backers were there and tackled him just short of the goal line. We had won, 34-33. The kids ran onto the field and celebrated, it was the third time this season the game was won, or for better words, preserved on the game's final play.

Week nine presented us with a tall challenge. Austin Lanier was having a great season, they were 7-1, and we knew they were good, but we wouldn't know just how good they were until after we played them.

Lanier's head coach Dennis Ceder had his boys ready. They came out fired up, and played very physical. They got after us, and we were never really able to establish any type of rhythm offensively.

They outplayed us in every phase of the game.

We were whipped 33-3.

If I ever had a moment in coaching I wish didn't happen, this was one of them.

Late second quarter, trailing by only seven and backed up inside our own ten yard line, our offensive coordinator, Ken Lloyd was attempting to go for it on fourth down and long yardage to go.

I was furious, Ken didn't know it was fourth down. He had lost track of the down and distance. Meanwhile a play was about to be run. I quickly ran to an official and called timeout.

I immediately got in Wayne's ear.

"Somebody down here has to know what the hell is going on," I said as I ran the punt team onto the field.

Ken was pissed, he came and found me.

"Mind your own damn business," Ken angrily yelled. "Why don't you try to stop the other team from scoring."

It was right in front of the kids on the sidelines, I was beyond angry. Why was he so mad at me? I wasn't the one who tried to go for it from our own eight yard line on 4th down. After Ken said some more things I really didn't want to hear, I paused and yelled back two careless and classless words.

"Fuck you," I said.

I knew that I was instantly wrong, but it was too late. I attempted to apologize at the half, but Ken didn't want to hear it. After the game I found Ken and told him that I was sorry and that I was wrong, I simply had lost my cool. He still didn't want to talk to me.

"I don't want to talk to you, leave me alone," Ken said. "I need some time to cool down."

I gave him some time, one week to be exact. A teacher who always sat in the first row of Travis football games reported my slip of the tongue; she had heard our verbal exchange.

I was in the wrong and should not have cursed at my fellow coach, but folks I have to be honest. I'm not trying to make an excuse, but coaching and cursing happens often and frequently during the course of football games. If you think it doesn't you are fooling yourself.

But I was going to be made example of, and I'm glad I was. The teacher reported the incident to our Principal. I was reprimanded, and ultimately told that I had to coach from the coaches' press box for the remainder of the season. I was devastated, and embarrassed.

From the press box I coached our regular season finale. If we won, we advanced to the playoffs.

We would be facing my former boss and friend Todd Patmon and the Reagan Raiders. Reagan was 1-8 and rumors were wildly spreading that Coach Patmon was going to be fired. Although I felt for Todd, I badly wanted to win this game. In many ways I felt that if I could beat my old boss, that I would win, on some kind of personal level.

It was a cold damp evening. The field was in terrible shape. The ground and the grass were both soaked. But the field's poor surface would not be a factor at all in our game.

The game was over quickly. We completely dismantled Reagan 42-6. We were in the playoffs. Just a year earlier I was on the Reagan sideline, and we had defeated Travis 47-14. How quickly things can change. We had turned the 2-1-27 Rebels into a winner. My friend Coach Patmon was fired the following week.

The playoffs were over before they started. Coach Lloyd was really upset that I was allowed to coach the Reagan game, and he would not let it go. He continued to voice his displeasure about that to me, Wayne, and anyone else who would listen.

"I don't think its right that you got to coach against Reagan," Ken said. "I just don't think its right."

Playoffs.

We faced an electrifying Pflugerville Connally team on a very cold and windy Friday night at the Palace in Round Rock.

They were very good, and featured several Division One players. Division One players are premium high school football players who are given scholarship money to attend football subdivision programs.

They crushed us: 63-14. Connally would advance to the State semi-finals, where they lost by a single point to the eventual Texas 4A State Champions.

Our season was over, it was time to get ready for spring football, or so I thought.

Not long after the season had ended David Seaborne, head coach at Austin LBJ was fired. His wife worked at Travis and I wanted to find her and somehow try to comfort her. I wanted her to know that I really liked David and thought that he was a good man.

Oddly enough, Coach Seaborne was hired at Travis as an assistant coach. We became friends instantly, and we talked about the great Reagan-LBJ games that we coached against each other.

"Those were incredible intense filled games," I said. "We were lucky to come out on top."

"I don't think luck had too much to do with it," Coach Seaborne said. "You guys (Reagan) were pretty good too." After getting to know him a little bit we frequently talked.

"What position are you going to be coaching?" I said.

"Defensive backs," Coach Seaborne said "What position do you coach?"

"Defensive backs," I quietly said, working hard to not show how awkward the moment was.

Inside my own body I screamed, I had to talk to Wayne.

"Is what David said true?" I asked.

"It is," Wayne said.

I was angry and confused. We had just gone 7-4, and I thought that I had played a large role in turning things around at Travis.

I expressed my thoughts to Wayne.

"I don't get it. We just had a really good season. I feel like I do a good job, and bring lots of energy to our practices." I said.

"I agree," Wayne said. "I totally agree. Sorry Coach, but it was a chance to get a former head coach on my staff, I'm still willing to keep you on as the head JV (Junior Varsity) coach."

I declined immediately. Call it pride or just flat out feeling betrayed, I let Wayne know that I would be leaving.

Ironically, Ken Lloyd was being offered a demotion as well.

Ken was much angrier than I was. The offense had had a pretty good season. We were the only two new additions to the varsity coaching staff in 2004, and had turned a 1-9 team into a 7-4 team overnight. We were both basically being let go.

Perhaps in a twist of fate, the two coaches who had cursed each other in week nine, now kind of rallied together. We weren't friends but understood that we were both getting a raw deal.

Ken and I talked often now, and although I had apologized profusely, I don't think he ever quite forgave me. During the course of one of our talks he made me think like I never had before. "You do a great job (of coaching), but maybe you push the players too hard." Ken said.

Next he said something that has stayed with me for the rest of my life.

"You are getting ready to be a father; would you want your kid to be coached by you?" Ken said.

I was stunned by how simple the question was and yet I knew the real answer. After a few seconds I replied.

"I don't know," I said. But I knew the real answer, it was no.

I was not mean or abusive in any way, shape or fashion towards my players. I simply cared way too much about winning and didn't model very good sportsmanship. and didn't model very good sportsmanship. I was mostly concerned about my use of profanity towards officials during the course of football games.

I thought for a long time about what Ken had said. I was going to be a better coach. I had decided that I was going to treat all players as if they were my own child. I constantly reminded myself that my players are someone's child, and are very special to someone.

Chapter 5

"Why are we here?" I asked the players.

"To be a better man," the players shouted back.

"What?" I asked.

"To be a better man," the players shouted louder.

"What is your job?" I asked.

"To love each other," the boys replied.

"I can't hear you," I said.

"To love each other," the boys roared back.

The sound was like a symphony to my ears.

This is how we start all of our meetings. By January 18, 2011, Boyz into Men was in full swing. We had established starting routines, developed our four rules, and developed a mission statement. We had already moved proverbial mountains in only two prior meetings. Football players were talking about their feelings and attempting to help others.

They were becoming men.

I made a decision that I was going to make sure the kids (football players) knew how much I loved them. I had to be willing to possibly be made fun of by my fellow coaches; in addition, the players might not buy into it. It was worth the risk, I always believed that you can never wrong a man who was in the right. I was inspired.

The inspiration came from an unlikely source. I say unlikely because it was given to me from someone I just didn't think cared much about me, my boss.

On December 14, 2010, Neal LaHue, the head football coach at Roosevelt, gave me a Christmas gift. It was a book, *Season of Life*, by Jeffrey Marx.

Our first three seasons together Neal and I had an up and down relationship at best. I think we were both mistrustful of each other. I was coaching defensive backs for him and at times I really didn't think he was happy with my performance, at least that was my perception. Mostly, I just flat out didn't think he liked me.

Neal, in a round-about way had inherited me from the former head football coach and had kept me on staff. But I always felt like he had viewed me as not 'one of his guys.'

Little did I know this book would help ignite the spark to better my relationship with him and countless others.

After reading *Season of Life* I felt like I had found my calling. I had to teach boys the proper way to be a man. The protagonist of the book, Joe Ehrmann, former Baltimore Colt star and volunteer high school football coach, teaches that men are often taught the wrong way to measure being a man. Coach Ehrmann simply believed that men don't have an understanding of what masculinity and manhood is. Joe Ehrmann also thought that in general men are victims of what he coined 'false masculinity.'

FALSE MASCULINITY: Athletic ability, sexual conquest, and economic success.

I was amazed at how accurate Joe Ehrmann's philosophy was.

I know that my idols, my heroes, people that I looked up to, certainly had fit all three of the criteria.

Hall of famer Mickey Mantle was a tremendous baseball player, but was a life-long alcoholic, who had widely publicized affairs with lots of other women outside of his marriage. And by all accounts, most importantly his own, he was not much of a father. He had made little effort to know his own children.

Yet, I looked up to him. But why?

It was obvious; it was because he was a great ball player.

I measured being a man on the ability to get base hits or hit homeruns. As a high school baseball player I remember feeling upset, absolutely crushed after going 2 for 3 (focusing solely on my strike out), like I had let the whole world down. I had made an out, I wasn't a real man.

The guys I wanted to be like in college were guys who were getting laid all of the time or who had nice sports cars. My fraternity brothers often came from money, and I wanted to be like them, a man.

"Masculinity, first and foremost, ought to be defined in terms of relationships," Joe said. "It ought to be taught in terms of the capacity to love and to be loved. If you look over your life at the end of it . . . life wouldn't be measured in terms of success based on what you've acquired or achieved . . . The only thing that's really going to matter is the relationships that you had . . . What kind of a father were you? What kind of a husband were you? What kind of a coach or teammate were you? What kind of a brother were you? What kind of friend were you?

I thought that Joe Ehrmann was, is, an incredible man. If I could somehow impact others the way he had done. I thought, *my life would be a success.*

However, Joe Ehrmann had the luxury of coaching at an elite private school, where they could teach about religion and God. They could also recruit and select who they wanted to play football. I did not have that luxury.

As much as I believed spirituality is an essential part of being a man, I had to shy away from it. I taught in a public school and I was not going to tell others who and what I thought they should believe in, at least not when it applied to religion. As a high school student and a history major in college I was familiar with the concept of separation of church and state. The concept refers to the distance in the relationship between organized religion and the nation state. The First Amendment states that "Congress shall make no law respecting an establishment of religion, or prohibiting the free exercise thereof."

I studied Joe Ehrmann's code of conduct that he used at Gilman High School and felt that I had to modify it slightly since I taught in a public school. Over the next few weeks, Boyz into Men had taken many of Joe's ideas and adapted them into concepts that I felt better suited Roosevelt High School. With the help of my football players, I developed the following:

OUR FOUR RULES TO GUIDE US

1. He accepts responsibility
2. He leads courageously
3. He helps others
4. He does the right thing

Chapter 6

"There is nothing quite like good barbeque," I told strong safety Joshua Glass, "and this ain't it." Joshua chuckled and continued to finish his brisket.

Joshua and I had good rapport, and I was proud of our relationship.

It was Wednesday, January 26, 2011. Joshua and I had just finished our workout in the Roosevelt weight room. We were hungry and I had promised him dinner.

I really liked Joshua, and saw enormous potential in him. I just hoped it wasn't too late in his life to tap into it. Although his actions and grades did not reflect it, Joshua was very intelligent.

Joshua had been in and out of trouble for as long as I had known him, even serving a two game suspension as a high school junior for violating team rules. He seemed to stay in trouble. For an assortment of reasons, he had numerous confrontations and blowups with several members of the coaching staff and other members of the faculty.

"Coach, the reason I have problems with those people is because of me, and I know I'm bad and sometimes do some stupid shit, but those people don't care about me so why should I listen to them," Joshua said. "I'm bad, I've always been bad, I don't really have a dad, and my mom is sick (breast cancer), so I just try to do what I can do to make it."

I paused and took a sip of my iced tea, then asked him a question.

"Do you really think you are bad?" I said.

"Coach, I know I am," Joshua said. "Do you remember last week's meeting (Boyz into men), when you asked us to raise our hands if we don't have a father. Well, I kind of told a lie. I do have a father. But the last time I saw him I was 14. When I told him that I was going to go stay with my mom because she was sick, he dropped me off and told me that I ain't shit, that I'm dead to him."

Joshua had bounced back and forth between his Mom and Dad his first fourteen years of life. Both of his parents spent multiple years in prison, with charges ranging from check fraud to possession of crack cocaine. While we sat down and shared a meal, we were actually sharing life. His story was very familiar to me. I related quite well to him, in particular his stories about feeling like he raised himself. He was wounded, and put up big walls around himself to shield himself from hurt. This particular evening we exchanged stories, mostly we just talked. Tonight I was more than his coach, I was his friend.

I felt for him, but I didn't want him to feel that it was okay just to do whatever he wants because of his challenging upbringing. I had felt sorry for myself for years, and it didn't help me.

In some ways, he reminded me of myself when I was his age. For a good portion of my life I had been raised solely by my father. My mother and father had a bitter divorce, and my father was awarded full custody of me. My mother would later be hospitalized in the Austin State Hospital for a wide variety of mental illnesses. Non-payment of child support often landed her short stays in the Travis County jail. I knew what it was like to hurt and miss a parent.

Physically, Joshua looked like a Greek God. His six foot-one inch frame and 193 pounds made me look even smaller than I already was. But when I looked at him, I didn't see a man, I saw a child.

As we finished our dinner and walked out of the restaurant Joshua stopped and looked at me for a second, as if sizing me up.

"Coach, I sign on Wednesday (National Signing Day), will you be there?" Joshua asked.

"Of course," I said. "I wouldn't miss it."

Just a day before National Signing Day (February 2, 2011) Boyz into Men held our weekly meeting. As an activity and as a way for me to learn more about the kids, they had to fill out a questionare that I had developed for them. One of the questions simply read:

What was the best day of your life, so far?

Joshua had left his blank, I asked him about it later in the hallway.

"Hey my man, why did you leave your sheet blank?" I said.

"I've never had a best day, except maybe when we beat MacArthur in overtime, but that only lasted for a few minutes," Joshua said.

I was saddened by his answer and hoped that things in his future might change for the better.

"Joshua," I said. "You are getting a scholarship, you hold the cards now. What you do with your life will be up to you. Do you understand me?"

"Yes Sir," he said, and continued to walk down the hallway.

National Signing Day.

In front of many of his peers Joshua signed his letter of intent to play college football at West Texas A&M. I brought my camera to take pictures of Joshua, Leland Young, and Quenton Bradley, who were also signing their scholarship papers.

I was so proud of the three of them. Leland and Quenton's families were taking pictures; I wanted to make sure that Joshua got a picture too.

"Can you take a picture of me and Joshua?" Joshua's mother said. "I left my batteries at home."

I had kind of anticipated that could happen and was really glad that I had brought my camera.

It was a fun morning, with a really neat atmosphere. Most of our varsity football team had come to watch the boys sign and to show their support.

The following week after having dinner at my house, Joshua and I were watching ESPN's Sports Center on the television. My wife, Mandy, had made us sloppy joes and some corn, so we 'could eat healthy.' Joshua and I both laughed as we went upstairs and said hello to my two daughters, Isabella and Ava, who were getting ready for bed. Isabella was six, and Ava was only two years old.

"Wow, he is big," Isabella said. "Is he a football player?"

I always worried about my children and the effect of my working seven day, 80-90 hour work weeks during football season. I know it was hard on my wife. Mandy and I often joked that she was a football widow during our season, but it was the truth. For four months out of the year she was in essence a single mom. I spent so much time and energy trying to help other peoples kids that I felt that I had neglected my own girls.

It is an awful feeling and one that I continue to struggle with. It has caused me much pain and moments of wondering why I do what I do. But it comes to this: my wife is able to stay at home and raise our children. Many of the boys that I coach have one or no parents. My girls have stability in their lives and most of the boys I coach have none. When I am home, or am lucky enough to spend time with Isabella and Ava, I shower them with love and affection. I make certain there is no doubt that they know I love them.

As Joshua lounged in the brown love seat, I stretched out on the floor. As I attempted to stretch my back and take a little pressure off my spine I had a question to ask him.

"Do you have a best day now?" I said.

Looking somewhat embarrassed he smiled.

"For sure, you know it," Joshua said.

Joshua Glass was an experiment of many sorts.

His first three years at Roosevelt he had been an outside linebacker.

Coach LaHue felt that he was a safety so that was where he was going to play his senior season.

"We don't have anyone else to play there, so let's just see how it goes," Coach LaHue said.

The experiment wound up working pretty well and Joshua blossomed into an all-district player under the direction of safeties coach Brett Griffin.

Joshua and I had grown fairly close over the past three seasons. Certainly as close as he was going to let anybody get to know him.

As a freshman he had been a big part of our 9th grade B team that went 10-0. I was their head coach and felt a great deal of pride that our 9th grade B team was undefeated and by in large crushed all ten of our opponents.

I gambled on Joshua. I truly cared for him and hoped that he knew it. After one of our football staff meetings one of my friends and fellow coaches had a few words for me.

"You had Joshua over at your house, are you crazy? You're wasting your time . . . I can't believe you let him around your kids."

I didn't know how to respond, so I just smiled and gave a quick, polite response.

"You might be right, but I'm going to try to help him." I said. "I see a lot of potential in him, and I like to think that maybe he can make something of himself."

I was hoping if Joshua was inserted into a leadership position, that maybe it could help him stay clear of trouble.

He became one the leaders in our Boyz into Men meetings. He shared often in our meetings, and was definitely not shy about voicing his opinion, if in agreement or disapproval.

During one of our many talks we had via cell phone, I had some questions for him. I fired away:

"Do you think Boyz into Men is a waste of my time? All of the other players I talk to say they really like Boyz into Men and that they are getting something out of it, do you get anything out of it? Does it help? Why do you come to our meetings?"

There was a long pause over the phone, and then he answered my questions like only Joshua could.

"Honestly Coach, I don't get a whole lot out of it, but I know that the other guys do. We talk about the shit that you bring up when we chill and shit on the weekends." Joshua said. "They're thinking about it, and trying to do right. But honestly, I'm from the streets . . . and this shit don't work where I come from. I come to the meetings because of you. You're the realest coach we got. I love you. You're my nigga', if any other coach was doing the meetings we wouldn't go."

I was flattered, and although he could not see me, I was smiling when I responded.

"Joshua, I'm not a nigger," I said. I knew that it was a compliment but I still was trying to work on him. He was going to need to sound scholarly at some point in his life.

"Coach J, you know what I mean," Joshua said. "You're my dawg, is that better?"

"That will have to suffice," I said.

Chapter 7

The Alonzo family had just finished a night of fun at the Wonder Lanes bowling alley. Sean Alonzo got into his mother's blue 2004 Hyundai. Sean's father, Michael, followed right behind them as they pulled out of the parking lot and headed east. It was late and it was time to go home. Passing abandoned warehouses and closed shops and restaurants they continued east on their journey home.

Wonder Lanes was a place where the Alonzo clan went often. They were avid bowlers and truly enjoyed family outings. The bowling alley, located on Austin Highway, was not far from their home, and less than five miles away from Roosevelt High School.

There were many stop lights on the way home. His father got in the left hand lane and rolled down his window, and shouted a joke in the direction of his wife and son, as he had done so many times before. Sean, Michael and Sandi, Sean's mother, carried on a conversation as they waited for each stop light to turn green.

At the intersection of Walzem and Mordred they stopped once again to joke and laugh with one another. This particular stop light was beyond familiar to the Alonzo's. Roosevelt High school sits there, and the Alonzo's had three sons who had played football for the Rough Riders. Michael had spent countless hours there: watching his sons play sub-varsity games, practice, or to check with teachers about the boys' progress in school.

After trading one more joke with Sean, Michael informed his family that he was going to stop at the Burger King and grab a burger. Sean told his father, "I'll see you at home."

Michael Alonzo rolled up his window and sped off. Sean watched the yellow 2001 Hyundai Tiburon until it was out of sight. He didn't know it would be the last time he would see his father alive.

Sandi and Sean made it home and parked, they lived in an area that when brand new had housed many young working class families. In the subsequent years it had become an area that was ridden with crime.

"My parents had lived there for nineteen years, it was once a good neighborhood, until all the Section 8 and Katrina (Hurricane Katrina) people moved in," said Sean Alonzo.

Section 8 move-ins had brought the value of the neighborhood down considerably.

Section 8, or the Housing Choice Voucher Program is a Federal program which provides housing assistance to low income renters and homeowners (To qualify for Section 8, you must be a low-income person)

"I don't know how it works, or how much they pay to live there. But man, there are a lot of Section 8's in my neighborhood," Sean Alonzo said. "We could have probably qualified for it, but my Dad didn't believe in taking handouts, he believed in working."

Your rent payment is based on your income. The voucher will pay anything above 30% of your adjusted monthly income, to an established limit. (For example, if you earn $2,000 per month and the

home you rent is $900 per month, you would pay $600 and the voucher would cover the difference)

Michael Alonzo pulled into his driveway and parked his car. From his bedroom Sean could hear the car's engine turn off, letting him know that his father was home. From the corner of his eye Sean saw a flash and heard a loud pop. Instantly, he knew it was a gunshot.

Sean ran to the front yard, almost flying as he got there, but was too late. His father had been murdered, a single gunshot to the head.

When our coaching staff heard about the Alonzo's loss, we worried deeply about Sean. Our first thoughts were: How was he doing? Would he quit football? Would he go down the dark path that so many had when dealing with such adversity?

But Sean is a strong young man, and not only responded well, but seemed stronger than ever.

Chapter 8

Jay Z's *Empire State of Mind* played loudly from our sideline. Our kids looked loose and confident. The defensive backs were moving to the beat as they went through our back pedal progression, our back pedal progression is a set of drills that we do every day that teaches proper footwork.When done over and over, muscle memory kicks in and the players can do it without really thinking about it.

While warming up the secondary, Coach Brett Griffin and I smiled at each other, and almost simultaneously said "we're going to win."

It was a rare occasion, we never got to listen to music during warm ups, but the Roosevelt cheer leading sponsor had found a way to bring some hip hop tunes and play them over the sideline speakers. While the Roosevelt cheer leaders stretched, the rest of the Roosevelt football team warmed up with their individual position coach.

It was nearly seven o'clock on Friday night, and you could feel the electricity in the air. It was October 1, 2010, and I stood standing beneath the big blue ocean of sky on the Heroes Stadium field turf, anxiously watching the clock, waiting for the game to start.

At seven thirty we would square off with the top ranked team in San Antonio, the MacArthur Brahmas, led by all-state tight end Jace Amarro. Rivals.com had rated him a 4 star recruit; he was highly sought after by many Division One colleges.

This game would be the one of the most memorable, emotionally charged games that I have ever coached in.

Game time.

After spotting MacArthur a quick 14-0 lead, we rallied. Led by Quarterback Sean Alonzo, Roosevelt took a 21-14 lead with just over two minutes remaining. Momentum swung in the Rough Riders favor after corner back Gerald Carson made a diving interception on a ball intended for Amarro.

But what looked like a game sealing play, was not. With only time for two throws into the end zone, the game looked decided. But after two very questionable pass interference penalties, MacArthur had one untimed down from the one yard line. Carson, who just a few minutes earlier was a hero, would be victimized on a perfectly thrown fade route into the corner of the end zone.

Overtime.

A coin flip decided who would get the ball first in overtime. Our defense huddled on the sideline; I met with the defensive backs. They were distracted and angry, still thinking about the two very questionable calls by the officials. Leland Young's brown eyes burned through his white face mask.

"Coach, they (the officials) won't let us win," Young said.

"We've already won; you're a winner, all of you." I said to him and the rest of the defensive backs. "Sometimes bad things happen for no reason, life is messy, and it's hard. Life, and this game, is not always a work of art. Men, we are going to win this game! I don't know how, but we are going to win. But, don't let this be the crowning moment in your lives. You don know it yet, but your lives are just beginning. Do you understand me?"

"Yes sir" the boys replied. Strong safety Joshua Glass looked at me with a perplexed look and an awkward grin.

MacArthur was awarded the ball first and scored rather easily. But their PAT attempt was no good as the holder bobbled the snap.

Our offense took the field. After three unsuccessful plays from scrimmage, we called a time out. We were facing fourth and a long seven from the Brahma twenty-two yard line.

Things did not look good for the Rough Riders.

The ball was snapped and the pass protection immediately broke down, Alonzo was forced to scramble and rolled to his left. He lofted a pass across his body in the direction of wide receiver Dominique Davis. Davis made an acrobatic catch and hauled it in at the twelve yard line giving us a new set of downs. It was a great throw and catch.

Somebody, somewhere, was looking out for us.

Alonzo would not be denied, plunging in from a yard out two plays later to tie the game. The PAT was next. I could barely watch. Kneeling on the sideline, I squeezed the hand of my two cornerbacks as we nervously watched the kick together. I felt as if my heart might explode out of my chest. Good snap, good hold, and the kick sailed through the uprights. It was good.

There was pandemonium on the field. I hugged everyone I could get my hands on. Offensive Line Coach Kevin Palmer actually picked me off the ground as he hugged me, as we exchanged congratulations. Defensive Line Coach Gene Scoggins gave me a big bear hug, with all 340 pounds of him holding me tightly. His shirt was soaked with heavy perspiration. He continued to embrace me.

"Unbelievable, un-fucking believable!" Gene said as he continued to squeeze me.

We had won, and fought our way through major adversity. We played with character, and as a team.

Nobody had turned on each other, or pointed any fingers. I was so proud of our team.

I found Sean Alonzo moments after the game had ended.

"Your father was watching, and he is very proud of you." I said.

Sean had been crying.

"I know coach, thank you." Sean said as he hugged me.

I held him for a few seconds as we enjoyed the moment. Television and newspaper reporters were coming in our direction.

"Coach, reporters," Sean said.

"They are not here for me Sean, they are here for you," I told him.

I watched him answer questions and tried to savor the feelings of jubilation that come with a great win.

Chapter 9

"Most kids at our school don't have fathers," Sean Alonzo said. "The person who shot my dad probably never had a father."

Sean's outlook on life amazed me. He always appeared to be upbeat, looking for ways to help others.

Sean credited his family for his strength. Sean, the youngest of six children, brought a lot of character and positive energy to Roosevelt.

For one, he was a natural leader. He also was very talented. He stood five foot-nine inches;one hundred seventy pounds of pure quarterback.

He played with guts, and lots of hustle. He outperformed more talented athletes.

Sean seemed unfazed by bad things that happened around him. I admired that quality about him. I was a Sean Alonzo fan.

Sean was our quarterback and unquestioned leader of our football team. When he spoke, kids listened. During the fall of 2010 he had put us on his back, leading us to many victories, and in to the playoffs.

Mostly, I think Sean wanted to be like any other high school athlete, but he wasn't.

"I miss my dad," Sean said. "I miss looking up into the stands and seeing him there."

With his father's name tattooed on his chest and R.I.P embroidered on his left cleat and DAD on his right cleat, in many ways his father is always with him on the football field.

Privately, Sean still struggles dealing with the tragic murder of his father.

"I still search for the shell casing in the front yard, wanting to find a clue as to why he was murdered," Sean said. "But there are no answers."

The Bexar County Sheriff's Department has been unable to solve the case, and the case remains unsolved. They continue to search for Michael's killer.

"I miss my dad, I miss his voice," Alonzo said. "I miss how much he supported me, he was fun. There is definitely a void now. But, I have to continue to fight. My dad wouldn't have wanted me to give up and quit; that's not how he raised me. He raised me to work hard. At one point he worked three jobs just to support us and keep our family going."

It is truly a gift when you get to coach young men with great competetitiveness, character, and a burning desire to succeed.

Thirteen days after the Roosevelt class of 2011 graduation, Sean and I met up for lunch.

I wanted Sean to know how proud of him I was.

Lunch.

We talked about his baseball scholarship to the University of Incarnate Word. We chatted about the College World Series. We both had teams we were rooting for. I was desperately hoping the Texas Longhorns would win it all; Sean was rooting for the Florida Gators.

I was curious as to his immediate plans and possible major.

"What do you want to do with your life?" I said.

"I want to go as far as baseball will take me. I might want to coach; I might want to be an athletic trainer. I know I want a family of my own when the time is right." Sean said. "I want to be sure that I can support them financially. I want what my parents had. My parents were great . . . are great. They had a really good-solid relationship."

Sean paused and tears swelled in his eyes.

"Sean we don't have to talk about this right now," I said.

I touched his knee under the table, trying to comfort him.

"It's okay man," I said.

I quickly changed the subject.

"Sean, you are going to love college." I said. "And the girls, there are girls everywhere. You are going to meet all different kinds of people, and make friendships that will last you your entire life."

We were having fun again.

We munched on our macho sized cheese burgers at Chris Madrid's. Chris Madrid's is a local San Antonio eatery that has great hamburgers and nachos.

Sean read the card I had written him.

It read:

Dear Sean,

I am very proud of you.
I think you are a great young man.
I love you.

Coach Jacobs

"Thank you Coach, I love you too," Sean said as he looked at me with a quick glancing smile.

I can hardly wait to know Sean as he gets older, pursues a career, and has a family of his own. I have no doubt that he will make a great father.

As strange as it might sound, I was proud of myself too. I had come a long way in the past several months, and there was definitely a time in my coaching career that there was no way I would have dreamed about doing what I now did on a daily basis: change lives.

I flashed back to my first year of coaching at Austin High.

I was very unsure of myself. I didn't have much of a clue yet about the kind of man that I wanted to be.

Did I have a special coach who had impacted me?

I did.

I attempted to reach Coach Bob Berger from my cell phone as I drove home. I had just exited Loop 410 when I gave up. His home phone continued ringing and ringing.He was not home.

Chapter 10

I thought about Coach Berger often, but rarely phoned him. Although he was retired now, he seemed to always be working. He was often working at one of Austin ISD's athletic facilities. He was the stadium supervisor at Burger Center (no relation). He was also in charge of putting on all of the districts track meets, as well as cross country events.

Coach Berger was a tall, tan athletic man in his early forties when I had first met him. His brown hair was doing its best to hide the grey that was beginning to set in. Coach Berger had come to Austin from the tiny west Texas town of Marfa, where he had lived and coached high school football.

Coach Berger had been there for me when I needed him in high school. Even if it was just to listen, he was there.

My father and step mother were good parents, we just didn't talk about anything outside of the box. Feelings, or for that matter, emotions were subjects that remained off limits. We definitely did not talk about family problems, and we certainly had our share of dysfunction.

My sister had run away from home when I was a sophomore in high school, and we didn't see her again for over a year. I assumed the worst. I quietly went about school and athletics and attempted to put on a 'happy face.' But I was lonely, and a good teacher could see it.

One day, my sister returned. She was nine months pregnant. Two weeks before I began my senior year, I was an uncle. I was seventeen years old.

Usually between seven o'clock and eight o'clock in the morning I would walk into Coach Stoeckle's room to get extra help with my algebra. Math was hard for me, so I did what I needed to do to fully understand it.

Coach Jerry Stoeckle was the golf coach at Austin High. He was also my algebra teacher. God Bless him, he was a patient man.

Coach Berger would spend many of his mornings in Coach Stoeckle's room. If he was going to be there, so was I. I found Coach Berger fascinating. He was often agitated, and came into the room just to gripe. I loved it. It was free amusement.

Coach Stoeckle was the polar opposite of Coach Berger. He was very calm, and his speech was very slow and deliberate. He was also a very poor dresser, often wearing tight green polyester pants accompanied by an equally hideous shirt. Coach Berger on the other hand spent a good deal of money on his wardrobe; he looked like a business man who belonged on Wall Street.

Coach Berger and Coach Stoeckle were close friends. At least two or three times a week Coach Berger would waltz into his classroom and instantly start griping, without really looking if anybody else was in the room. Although it took him some time Coach Berger learned to scan the room first before he started on his daily 'bitch session.'

"Good morning Ben," Coach Berger said. "Can you step out of the room for a minute; I need to talk to Coach."

"Yes Sir" I said.

After a few weeks Coach Berger had progressed to 'Ben, cover your ears.' After a few months he just talked about whatever he was going to talk about. Occasionally, he would give me a stern look, and say 'this is not to be repeated, do you understand?'

By the spring semester I no longer needed help in algebra. I continued going to Coach Stoeckle's room. I enjoyed hanging out with them. It probably annoyed them that I hung out there almost every morning, but they never said a word about it. They made me feel good. Mostly, I just wanted to hear Coach Berger complain about something. He had a way to make it sound like he was right every single time. I thought Coach Berger was a pretty cool guy, plus he drove a silver Corvette.

Football.

Coach Bob Berger was extremely hard on me, I often dreaded going to football practice. He pushed me, harder than I wanted to be pushed. In his own words, he could be an 'ass hole.' But it was what I needed. I played best when I was angry. For whatever the reason, I focused better.

I had caught several balls the night before, highlighted by a thirty-five yard fade route against the second ranked team in the state. A fade route is a passing play where the receiver fades to the sideline and the quarterback throws a pass over his outside shoulder. We had lost 14-0, but I was pretty pleased with myself. My good feelings would not last long.

"Nice fucking block sweet pea," Coach Berger said. "If you don't block, you won't play."

I didn't understand, *wasn't my job to catch footballs?* After being ridiculed during Saturday morning film I was close to tears. Saturday morning film is when you watch Friday night's game and see what you did well, and what you need to fix.

I had quite a bit to work on. Coach Berger was right, I hadn't blocked a soul.

Within a few weeks I was arguably one of the best blockers on the team. My blocks would often spring our tailbacks for long runs resulting in touchdowns.

During our football game versus Round Rock High School I had sustained a deep cut to my left calf muscle. I was forced to come out of the game and get bandaged up.

At half-time Coach Berger came over and looked at me while the trainer reinforced the giant bandage and put a fresh layer of tape on me.

"What the hell is a matter with you?" Coach Berger said. "Just rub some dirt on it; you'll be alright sweet pea."

I hated him, and I loved him.

Coach Berger and I kept in touch throughout my college years.Occasionally I would drop by Austin High every now and again to say hello, and let him know how I was doing.

As an adult I got to know him. Eighteen years later we still talk on the telephone, laughing and exchanging the stories of our lives.

Chapter 11

	District 25-5A					
	District Overall					
	W	L	W	L	PF	PA
AUSTIN	0	0	5	0	273	0
Westlake	0	0	5	0	267	64
Hays	0	0	4	1	126	47
Seguin	0	0	2	3	99	159
Crockett	0	0	1	4	88	167
Bowie	0	0	0	5	60	151

"You better get to the stadium early, Austin High's offense is lethal, they put points on the board, they burn light bulbs out."

My first year of coaching high school football was 1999. My former coach, Bob Berger, had arranged to get me an interview with the principal. My interview went well, and within a few minutes I would be offered a job teaching special education at my alma mater, Stephen F. Austin High school in Austin, Texas.

Austin High is the oldest public high school in the state of Texas. It serves a variety of different families, form very wealthy to low income. Former President

George W. Bush's two daughters attended Austin High when I first started coaching.

I thought, *not every high school has secret service agents in the hall.*

I thought Austin High was a unique, special place. We had a culturally diverse student population.

Founded in 1881, Austin High is the oldest public high school west of the Mississippi River.The current campus, the one that I attended, is located near down town Austin. It hugs Town Lake. In 1953, Austin High was renamed Stephen F. Austin, after the settler who was credited with finding the state of Texas.

Shortly after my hire date, the head football coach at that time, Mickey Moss, had an opening on his staff and offered me a job coaching defensive backs. I reluctantly accepted. At this point in my life I just wasn't sure if I was ready to commit to the kind of hours that a coach has to work. I still had some partying I had to get out of my system.

As a college student I was what a lot of people call a 'party guy.' Friday nights were my night to go out and have fun, which for me (at this stage in my life) meant womanizing and often consuming large quantities of alcohol. Obviously those nights would be coming to a screeching halt. Well, at least for a while.

The season began with a loss to a very talented Round Rock McNeil team. We won our next two games, but they were dogfights.

We really struggled and we finished 3-7. We simply could not move the football and were in the wrong offensive scheme. We were based out of a wing set and running the veer with minimal success.

A single-wing is any offensive formation with exactly one wingback and one tight end aligned together.The veer is an option running play, in which the quarterback reads the defensive end. In theory, the veer is an effective ball control offense that can help minimize physical mismatches. However, in our case, it seemed to lead to an excessive amount of turnovers.

One of the bad parts about coaching is that you are unfortunately measured on wins and losses, and that grown men who have families to support, get fired.

Coach Moss informed the offensive coordinator that he was going to make a change. It was the right move. He hired offensive coordinator Chris Wood who installed a no huddle, spread offense that was fun to watch and equally fun to coach. Coach Wood wound up staying at Austin High for only one season. He returned to Arkansas where he was named head coach at Shiloh Christian, where he would win a state championship.

The 2000 season was one of the most fun and joyful years of my career. We were picked to finish last in our district by the local media; I guess you could say they were wrong.

We opened the 2000 campaign with a team we knew well, the McCallum Knights. Kickoff was set for Friday, September 8, 7:30.

It was a gorgeous September evening, and we were playing at one of my favorite stadiums, House Park.

House Park is the home stadium for Austin High, as well as Anderson, McCallum, and Lanier High schools. Built in 1939, just down a steep hill from the old Austin High, it had been dedicated to the memory of Austin High students who had lost their lives serving in World War I.

House Park had been built on land donated by Mr. Edward House, a former diplomat and advisor to President Woodrow Wilson.

Another thing that set House Park aside from most other high school football stadiums is the fact that it does not have a running track around it. The fans are almost right on top of the players. Playing there is an intimate experience. You can actually smell the fans popcorn from the sidelines;it was a neat venue to coach at.

We routed McCallum 48-0 to open the season. Using our newly installed no huddle, wide open passing attack, we sacked the Knights.

It was hard to believe that we had finished 3-7 just a season ago. While our offense piled up the yards and points, our defense provided its own highlights. Our defense scored two touchdowns and dominated McCallum's rushing attack.

The opener was a sign of things to come. The next four weeks we continued to play stellar football. After five games we had outscored our opponents 273-0. We had literally burnt out some of the bulbs on the House Park Stadium scoreboard.

We were 5-0, undefeated and unscored-upon. We had not given up a point all season!

The stage was set for what many of the local news stations were calling 'The battle of the Titans.'

We had a date with Austin Westlake. Westlake was ranked #1 in the State, and was also ranked #3 in the USA Today's Super 25 national poll.

The entire city of Austin was talking about our upcoming matchup with Westlake. People who I had not heard from in months were calling me and leaving long detailed voice messages on my phone: "Can you get me a ticket? Can I watch from the sideline?"

Both teams were undefeated. It was the District 25-5A opener. It was the only game played on this particular Thursday night.

House Park was completely sold out. All 6,186 seats were taken. The Austin High side sold out about thirty hours before game time.

At least three hundred fans lined the embankment of the 15th Street bridge. Approximately three hundred more had gathered along the fence just south of the scoreboard. The stands were packed. They were overflowing.

"I've never seen anything like it," the assistant Austin Independent School District athletic director said. "I've been here about thirty-four years, and I can't remember the last time there was a sellout of a high school football game."

Unfortunately, the game did not live up to the hype.

Westlake took the game's opening kickoff, and in just nine plays moved the ball seventy-four yards to score a touchdown, snapping our scoreless streak. Our spirits were broken as well. We lost badly, 56-6. Even when we knew the exact play they were going to run, it didn't matter. Westlake scored on its first five possessions.

We could not stop them. We were beaten like a drum. There was a reason they were ranked #3 in the nation.

Westlake would not lose a game until the State Championship; where they lost a hard fought 35-21 contest to Midland Lee. Midland Lee was led by tailback Cedric Benson, future Texas Longhorn and first round draft pick of the Chicago Bears.

The next week we responded by beating Austin Bowie 31-23, but it was a costly victory for the Austin Maroons.

Our quarterback, Stephen Kelley, had been injured and would be lost for the remainder of the season. We barely held on, nearly letting a 31-7 lead escape us. Bowie had two future stars in University of Texas Longhorns Michael and Marcus Griffin. Michael would later be a star in the National Football League, blossoming while playing safety for the Tennessee Titans.

We finished the season 8-3, bowing out in the first round of the 5A Texas high school playoffs, losing to San Antonio MacArthur. Class 5A is the highest classification of football in the state of Texas. Classification is based on student enrollment; any high school that has more than 2,085 students plays in class 5A.

It was a huge season for me personally as I formed meaningful relationships with my fellow coaches and players. I was hooked; I knew I was a coach.

After the game ended, we shook hands with our opponents. I looked up into the stands one last time as our loyal fans, sporting Maroon T-shirts exited the Alamodome seats. It was my first time to be in the playoffs, and I wanted to soak up the experience.

Several of our players were crying as Coach Moss addressed the team for one final team talk. For our seniors, their high school playing days were over.

They were hurting and I didn't quite know how to help them. I was ill equipped. I felt for them, I told them that I was proud of them and gave them a pat on the butt.

I wanted to hug them, but didn't. I was afraid of what the other coaches might say; mostly I was afraid that they would think I was soft and not a real man.

The 2001 season was equally fun, and we were just as good, maybe even better. Once again we started the season 5-0.

Week Six matched us with a familiar foe; it was our nemesis, Austin Westlake. Only this time Westlake was not ranked #1 in the State. They were #2.

Austin High was decked out in our traditional away white jerseys with solid white pants. The entire season we wore a special decal commemorating our 100 years of football anniversary season. Normally, we wore maroon helmets with just a white *A* decal in the middle of it. This one season there was a football fused into the *A*, with *100years* burned into it.

We jumped ahead 7-0, and were driving with a chance to make it 14-0, when the wheels completely fell off the wagon. Quarterback Nathan Kreutz fumbled and Westlake recovered at their own seven yard line. Led by future Texas A&M products Chad Schroeder and Joey Thomas, the Chaps scored forty-nine consecutive points and routed us by a score of 49-22.

Sometimes you can let a loss linger and beat you for another week. Week two of district play matched us against a very talented Austin Bowie team, once again led by Michael Griffin. We played in a daze for two and half quarters. After trailing 34-7 midway through the third quarter we caught fire and scored twenty-one consecutive points to cut the lead to 34-28.

But the Bulldogs would score twenty-nine consecutive points and beat us 63-28. We were now 5-2, 0-2 in District play. If we lost again we would be eliminated from any playoff scenarios. We would have to win out.

Things did not look good for the Austin High Maroons. We had to play Buda Hays at Bob Shelton stadium, which is not an easy place to play at. The game was nearly sold out and buzzing with excitement.

There was also a large group of people protesting outside Shelton Stadium. The large group took issue with the University Interscholastic Leagues executive committee's ruling to ban the use of the confederate flag. The Hays mascot was a Rebel, and the confederate flag was on their helmets as a decal. Many people found the Rebel flag offensive, they commented on the local news stations that 'it was a reminder of when slavery ruled the South.'

Having already given up a touchdown pass on a wild deflection on the final play of the first half and having two touchdowns called back on controversial calls, the Maroons showed a lot of fight in pulling out an exciting 35-28 come from behind win. With one minute and fifteen seconds to play, quarterback Trey Grady drove the Maroons ninety-three yards for the winning score.

Grady would hit wide receiver Raphael Hearne for the game winning 61 yard touchdown pass with forty-eight seconds remaining.

We still had to win our final two games to get into the playoffs. Next up was Austin Crockett. Crockett provided little resistance. After spotting Crockett an early 7-0 lead; the Maroons easily defeated the Cougars 55-7. Our quarterback duo of Trey Grady and Nathan Kreutz continued to be effective as they passed and ran for a combined 324 yards. The following week Austin faced the Seguin Matadors. On a very cold and windy night, the defense played extremely well. The Maroons blanked the Matadors 21-0 and clinched a playoff spot.

The following week our season would be over. We finished the season 8-3, losing to San Antonio Madison in the first round of the playoffs. Madison was loaded with talent: University of Oklahoma tailback Jacob Gutierrez, University of Kansas tailback Gary Green, University of Baylor cornerback Anthony Arline.

We simply could not stop them. They were a much better football team than we were.

Once again our seniors stood weeping on the soggy natural grass field that was doing its best to repel the rain it had encountered. We had played Madison at a neutral site, Smithson Valley High School. Coach Moss hoped that the grass field would slow the Mavericks down.

"We don't want to play them on turf," Coach Moss said. "They have too much team speed." But I don't think it did anything. I felt that it had almost no impact on our game. Well, I take that back, it did accomplish one thing: it got everyone muddy, no one was spared.

One of my all time favorite players, Andrew Collins, just stood there, staring at the score board as if somehow we could get a 'do-over.'

Andrew was special to me. I had watched him mature right before my eyes. His grandfather had died during the 2000 season, and I was impressed at how he battled through his pain. Also, after my engagement to my wife, as a gift to me, he serenaded us with her favorite song: *Still Remains* by the Stone Temple Pilots. Andrew's real passion was music; football was just something he did because it was fun. He was a great player, and a neater person.

He could not believe that we had lost, and he continued to weep.

I attempted to console him, but my words did little to comfort him. I embraced him, we hugged for what felt like an eternity; he would not let go. Someone from the press took a picture of that moment. The picture remains on my desk to this day. During the past two seasons Andrew and I had formed a bond. I didn't know it yet, but that is what high school football should be all about, loving your players and teaching them how to love one another.

Whispers filled the Austin High coaches' office. Coach Moss had not been in his office for a few days, but to be perfectly honest, I hadn't really noticed. I was still a newlywed, and at this point in my marriage every day was like Christmas. I couldn't wait to go home and see my wife at the end of a long, hard work day.

Rumors had spread through the hallways at Austin High School, "Coach Moss is leaving."

I asked one of my fellow coaches if the rumors were true. He was pretty sure that they were true. I didn't want to believe it.

The following day Coach Moss was back at work and called me into his office mid-morning. He informed me that he was accepting the head football coach position at South Garland High School. He thanked me for my efforts and before I knew it he was on his way.

Austin High had just come off of consecutive 8-3 seasons, and Coach Moss was a hot name in the world of Texas high school football. He had turned Austin High around.

Austin High had had only one winning season since 1978 prior to 2000. I, more than many, knew just how far our program had come. As a player, I was a part of the losing seasons.

Like all levels of football, (high school-professional) when a head coach is successful, he often leaves for perceived to be better or more lucrative job offers.

This is when I learned that being a football coach while waiting for the next coach to be named your future boss is not a very good time in one's life.

Our entire staff supported and rooted for David Hoff, a long time coaching veteran and great man. He was our assistant head coach and was very knowledgeable.

But in my mind, the very influential Austin High booster club, as well as the brand new school principal already had someone in mind. I believed that they wanted a bigger, more successful name.

They decided on Steve Davis from Austin Westlake, their offensive coordinator. The move certainly made sense in many ways; Westlake was coming off consecutive state runner-up finishes and did have an excellent program. We certainly had not been able to find a way to beat them. I don't have a negative thing to say about Steve, he always treated me fairly and with respect. He offered me a job, and perhaps I should have accepted.

But I was young, and had never been through the experience before. I didn't handle it (the transition) very well.

I was extremely upset that Coach Hoff did not get the job and voiced my displeasure with the Principal. I felt that she had completely disregarded my opinion as well as everyone else on the football staff. I very childishly let her know that I was beyond hurt, and that I was going to resign.

She could care less. She had little to no problem accepting my letter of resignation, and I was too prideful to ask for my job back. I had been married less than a year, and was now jobless.

Chapter 12

As the boys shuffled into our first ever Boyz into Men meeting music from my iPod filled the team room. Lionel Ritchie's *'You are the Sun, You are the Rain'* played as the last of the boys sat down and grabbed the piece of paper that was placed on their chairs.

I had asked the boys to write down what they thought the definition of a man was. I was amazed at how many of them left it blank.

"It's too hard Coach," said one of the boys.

"I don't get it Coach," a different football player said.

"I don't get it either, is this a trick question?" said another young man.

I chuckled quietly and repeated the question, "What makes a man a man?"

"There is no right or wrong answer," I said with a slight grin. "I just want to know what you think. Be prepared to explain your answer."

During our first ever character education meeting I had found a way to spark their interest with one simple question: What makes a Man a Man?

I was amazed and actually impressed with many of the boys' answers. Quite a few of them were light years ahead of me when I was their age.

I had anticipated many of the answers that I got:

"He has a big house" said one of the boys.

"He is a ladies' man" offensive lineman Evander Gomez said, giggling softly.

"He is a good football player. He played college or pro ball," said one of my Defensive Backs.

"Okay," I said.

"He helps others" said backup line backer Christian Pastrano.

"Good answer," I told him. "What do you mean? Could you tell me more?"

"Well Coach, I mean a real man is someone who thinks of others first. Someone who isn't afraid to do the right thing. Does that make sense Coach?"

"It does Christian, thank you," I said. I thought to myself, *Wow, I found a leader.*

The group was interested and somewhat intrigued. Now I would stick my claws in them.

Just a few weeks earlier when I had done some soul searching looking at myself in the mirror, I had made my mind up that I was going to make a difference in our boys lives.

I thought that if they could see my life through my eyes and my experiences; that this group (Boyz into Men: Character Education) had a chance to work, and not only work, but to change lives.

They were going to see me not just as a football coach, but as a man.

A man that has flaws, and is flawed. A man that has problems, a man that has struggled with his own demons and issues resulting from a challenging upbringing.

"I'm going to tell you what I think a man is, and should be. The measure of a man ultimately comes down to the relationships you've made with others. You have to let people in to your life. Once they are in, now there is a chance to love and be loved," I said. "All of you are in. If you are here, then you are in. I love all of you."

I knew that I might catch some flack about sharing too much personal information about myself. I just didn't care about any possible ramifications. I wanted genuine-authentic relationships with the boys in my group, and that was only going to happen with complete honesty.

I shared my life story. I wanted them to see me for who I was: I was a son, I was a father, I was a husband I was a man who had been hurt.

"Being a football coach does not encompass me." I said. "I'm a person made of flesh and blood. I'm a man." I was a lot more than just someone who taught them how to backpedal and read routes. I had been in their shoes and I wanted them to understand that.

Visible, by our projector, the power point read:

Coach Jacobs' testimonial

*Violence (History)
*Alibi for excuses, family issues
*Speech problems
*Shame (Jail)
*Accept Responsibility

I was somewhat nervous as I covered each topic. My stomach was churning and I could hear my voice tremble ever so slightly. But the more I talked about each topic, the more I shared, the better I felt.

Violence, I had seen it as a child. I knew the effects it had on people. Once, while visiting my uncle, my mother and I had gotten to my uncle's apartment just moments after he had stabbed his wife in a lover's rage with a kitchen knife. I was petrified that my uncle would come after me. I spent many years scared, and slept with a baseball bat as protection until I was eleven years old.

I shared my deepest, most shaming facts about myself. I was vulnerable.

My mother and father divorced when I was five years old. From age 6 to 8 I was able to see my mother every other weekend as per court order. I missed my mother. When I did stay with her on the weekends it was not terribly uncommon for me to accompany her to nightclubs or bars. I didn't know that it was wrong to sleep at bars or night clubs as a child while my mom was having fun or working.

My mother could not afford to pay the child support that she owed my father. She was often arrested for failure to comply with the court. I developed a chip on my shoulder. I was heart-broken and ashamed.

I was ashamed of many things, mostly that my mother bounced around from one run down east side apartment to the next. I was ashamed that she lived in a trailer. I was ashamed that my mother had spent time in the Austin State Hospital. I was ashamed that my mother had married four times. I was ashamed that my father had married three times. I was ashamed that my sister had dropped out of high school and had three children out of wedlock before the age of twenty-one. I was ashamed and embarrassed that I had a stutter.

I was ashamed. I was angry with the world. *Why me?* I thought. *Why me?*

I made it perfectly clear to my audience that when I went to college I used my pain and feelings of shame to justify some pretty bad behaviors. I explained to the group that I used my childhood (things that I didn't like) to feel sorry for myself. I had used them as fuel for my fire. I made excuses for myself. I felt like I was a victim. I drank beer in college, and lots of it. I was a womanizer; sleeping with women was a temporary way to make myself feel happy. I did it frequently. I thought that the more women I could have sex with, the closer I might become to being a real man. Mostly, I refused to feel pain. I had put big walls up around myself, and I thought I could ease the pain with alcohol and women. I was wrong.

Months before I had met my wife I realized that I had some problems. I was tired of staying out late, drinking, and chasing after women. As an assistant coach at Austin High I still went out almost every Saturday night. After spending a night in jail, I decided I had felt sorry for myself long enough. I was twenty-five years old.

I accepted responsibility for my actions. It was not anybody's fault that I made poor choices in college other than my own. I was responsible. No more excuses. I was going to do my best to deal with my issues and my feelings of shame in a more productive way.

"Bad things are going to happen, and you have to do your best to deal with them," I said. "If you accept defeat, that's exactly what you'll get."

I wanted my group, Boyz into Men, to know that I had made some terrible choices as a college student and as a new teacher. I wanted them to learn from my experiences. "I did the wrong thing for a long time," I told them. "But now, I'm right."

I wanted to give them a more concrete example.

I reminded the group about the terrible stutter I had as a child. Well, I said, "I actually still have it, I'm just a lot more comfortable with the fact that I am a stutterer and that I have days when words are hard for me. If someone is going to laugh at me for that, than they are the one with a problem, not me."

I was completely vulnerable. My honesty and sincerity gave me instant credibility with the kids. I already had a good-solid relationship with most of the boys. But, I needed to touch their souls. I felt that I had accomplished my mission for the day. We had made a connection.

I instructed the young men that accepting responsibilitywould be the first of our four rules.

After a brief pause we did a bit of a social experiment. I asked the boys to raise their hand if they had ever been told that men are not supposed to cry. All sixteen of the boys raised their hand. I asked them to stop and take a look at one another. I explained to the group that we often don't know how to be men because we have never been taught. We are often told to 'be a man' without really knowing what that meant.

"Well that's a bunch of crap," I said. "Men have to learn how to feel, how to cry, and how to love. We don't know how to have healthy relationships with each other. You are going to learn how to love yourself and each other."

After I dismissed the boys to go to their first period class I expected to hear giggles or snickering as they left the room.

But that didn't happen. Instead, many of them stayed and asked me questions.

Christian Pastrano shook my hand as he left the team room. "See you next week Coach." He said, "I'll be back."

Chapter 13

I had just taken a sip of my frozen lime margarita when my cell phone rang. The salt rimmed glass stung my chapped and cracking lips. I really didn't want to answer my phone. I really liked margaritas, and Pappasitos made one of the best in Austin.

I had arranged to leave school early and meet my wife for 'dinner and drinks.' It had been a challenging week at Reagan High School, and I wanted a little relaxation. I didn't have an eighth period class and I didn't have any papers to finish grading. I grabbed my bag and headed for the parking lot. It was a Friday, and it was hot. The steering wheel burned my fingers as I started the engine.

My cell phone continued to vibrate as it moved ever so slightly on the table. 'Incoming call, incoming call,' echoed my cell phone.

"Are you going to get it?" asked my wife.

"What?" I said.

"Your phone," she said. "Are you going to answer it?"

I really did not want to answer my phone, I just wanted to relax and enjoy a good meal. *I better get it,* I thought, *it might be one of my players.* I always prided myself in being available to my players. Hesitating, I flipped the phone open and answered.

An excited voice immediately started talking.

"Do you have any idea what just happened here?"

"No," I said.

"You're not going to believe this shit," linebackers coach Brian Mattingly said. "Marcus (McTear) just killed his girlfriend."

"Oh my God," I replied. "Where?"

"At school man! You need to get down here."

Apparently, just after 4pm, Eve Daniels had been standing upstairs in the main walkway of Reagan's New Mall. The New Mall was the newer of two school buildings that sported outdoor courtyards. It was there that McTear approached her, allegedly armed with two large knives. He brutally stabbed her to death.

Autopsy report.

Eve was stabbed six times: once through the chest; piercing her heart, once through the back, piercing her left lung; once through the top of her skull, penetrating her brain; and once on either side of the head, each thrust entering her brain through the temporal lobe.

I slid my glass away from me and towards my wife.

"We have to go," I quietly said.

"What's wrong?" Mandy said.

"One of our players just killed somebody," I said. "You're going to need to get the check. I need to go."

I wandered out to my car and started the engine. The Mustang's engine started with a loud purr, I immediately turned the air conditioner on. The cold air hit me like a ton of bricks. I paused and looked at my watch, it was 4:44. I turned off the engine and headed back to the restaurant.

I quickened my step; Mandy had just paid the bill when we almost ran into each other as I entered the restaurant. The smell of refried beans and grilled chicken fajitas filled the air, but I had no appetite.

"I need you to drive," I said. "We're going to leave my car here."

Quickly we piled into my wife's 2000 Jeep Grand Cherokee. We were only about a mile away from Reagan. We were there in no time. As she parked her car, we both had noticed the small fleet of police cars that were in the parking lot.

"Do you think it's safe?" She asked.

I didn't respond.

I thought to myself, *is it ever?*

I turned and looked out the window, local news stations were setting up their cameras.

Chapter 14

I was absolutely thrilled when I was hired as defensive coordinator at Austin Reagan. The Reagan Raiders had recently hired a new head football coach, Todd Patmon. Todd was a handsome twenty-nine year old Black man who had coached defensive backs at Desoto, Texas. He was young, and I was a year younger than he was. He was soft spoken with a mild sense of arrogance about him. I liked him instantly.

I thought he was just what Reagan needed, a young strong black male. Reagan was on the East side of Austin, our school racial demographics were: 53% Hispanic, and 43 % Black. Many of our students lived at or below the poverty line. Our school enrollment was right around 1,200 students. Although it seemed like no more than 1,000 students ever actually attended. We had only three White players in our entire football program.

Austin Reagan had a long standing tradition of winning in high school football. They had won the State championship three times, and was a school that was often feared by its opponents. I hoped I wouldn't be the guy who screwed it up.

I was hired in mid-June and immediately went to the weight room to eye ball the kids I would be coaching. They certainly passed the eye ball test. Mostly, I was impressed by how hard they worked. The weight room was full, and the sound of rap music roared out into the hallway. I was home.

Potentially, I thought we could be very good. We had athletes, and we had good team speed. What we did not have was an offensive line. We would need to be creative and be smart with our blocking schemes.

We lost our season opener to the Burnet Bulldogs. Burnet was an absolutely spectacular football team, but we should have beaten them. They were led by two incredible players: quarterback Stephen McGee and wide receiver Jordan Shipley.

Shipley would re-write the Texas high school football statistical record books. He also starred at the University of Texas. Currently, Shipley is a wide receiver for the Cincinnati Bengals.

Not to be totally outshined by Shipley, McGee starred at Texas A&M and in 2010 started two games for the Dallas Cowboys.

Burnet would win its first fifteen games of the 2002 season.

It was a hard hitting defensive struggle for three quarters, with us trailing 7-6. The fourth quarter was simply all Burnet, mostly it was all Shipley. They scored twenty-six points in the game's final quarter and as defensive back Roderick Mosely said "that (Shipley) might be the fastest white boy I have ever seen." The 33-6 score was not indicative of how well we played defensively.

Defensively we were based out of a 3-4 front and mixed zone and man coverages, obviously not well enough. The 3-4 defense is made up of three defensive linemen and four linebackers.

We had given up a punt return to Shipley for Burnet's first score, and had turned the ball over seven times, putting our defense in numerous binds.

In the fourth quarter Shipley returned an interception for a touchdown, scored on a reverse, and threw a touchdown. He was all over the place, and was by far the best player on the field. It was the first time I had ever witnessed one player basically win a game all by himself.

We had little time to feel sorry for ourselves. The Leander Lions loomed ahead. They were a big and very physical 5A football team. We knew we were going to be in for a fist fight of a game. Once again, our defensive unit played quite well, limiting a very potent offense to less than 240 yards. We played a 4-2-5 against the Lions all night. We slanted often. They had not anticipated this and it really gave their offensive line problems. A 4-2-5 is a defense that consists of four defensive linemen, two linebackers and five defensive backs. I liked the 4-2-5 because it gave me four true down linemen and five defensive backs to help defend against passing offenses. A slant is when you move your defensive line either away or towards whatever side you have declared the strong side.

Leander benefited from two turnovers, and two blocked punts. Like the previous week, our lone score would come from a punt returned for a touchdown. Final score: Leander 21—Reagan 8.

We were 0-2 and really struggling, internally and on the scoreboard. Players were beginning to question and argue with each other and with the coaches. Coach Patmon was getting ugly phone calls that he had ruined the program and that he should leave town.

I promised our players that if we stuck together and kept working that things would turn around for us. I was searching for something, anything that might get the kids to loosen up, relax and just play football. David Teaney, one of our linebackers, and (one of only three white players on our team) was enjoying the little bit of scruff that was on my chin. He thought that I would look pretty funny with a beard. Without really thinking,

I promised him and the rest of the guys that I would not shave again unless we lost.

It would be a long time, and I would get very itchy.

Our next opponent was Lampassas. Lampassas is a small town in Lampassas County, Texas. The 2000 census report put the population at 6,786. The racial makeup of the city was 84.78% White, 2.03% African American. We found our entire experience in Lampassas unpleasant.

Once again we played great defense and won an intensely physical game 8-6. It was not a thing of beauty like the score suggests. But it was a win, and we needed one. A couple of things happened that night in Lampassas that would help make the season become very special.

Mainly, we became a team.

We were housed in a locker room about the size of a storage shed. It was insanely hot; temperatures were well over 110 degrees. It blew my mind that there was not even a fan in our locker room. Our players and coaches rallied together. Although it was probably unintentional, we had believed we were being discriminated against because we were a predominantly African American football team, coached by a predominantly African American staff. After several questionable calls not going our way and our opponents using racial slurs through all four quarters, we did manage to escape with a victory. As our charter bus pulled out, I remember an object being thrown at our bus, and "go home niggers" being yelled out. I don't want to indict a whole town because of the actions of a few, but we were glad to be leaving. After all the kids had left to go home, I remember asking Coach Patmon to write a letter to their head coach about the treatment of our players.

"Ben, I probably won't write him," Coach Patmon said. "What would I say, some people are just ignorant."

Week four had us matched up against the Lockhart Lions. On the opening kickoff Paul Darby Jr., knocked out the kick returner; he was out cold. It set the tone for the entire game. We won 35-0. Our players were physically superior. We were a physical team, and we continued to put bone-jarring hits on the opposing team. I felt for their kids, and hoped that no one else from their team would get hurt. It's a strange feeling as a coach and as a man that as you want your team to win, and win big, but at the same time feel badly for your opponent.

"Get a Jaguar," Black Cory shouted.

"Reagan Raiders," the rest of the team sounded off, almost in perfect unison.

"Get a Jaguar," Black Cory once again shouted.

"Reagan Raiders," the rest of the team responded.

Everyone (the student body) at Reagan High School called him Black Cory, but his real name was Cory Cameron. Cory had gotten his nickname because his skin was very dark. Cory was the center on our football team, and a fierce competitor.

Our team had gathered at midfield, in an attempt to intimidate our bitter rival, Austin LBJ.

In addition to the usual excitement that surrounded the district opener for both teams, an incident had happened the night before that had our players revved up and ready to go. We were practically chomping at the bit.

Somebody, we assumed from LBJ, had broken into Nelson Field and had spray painted LBJ in big purple letters near the fifty yard line the night before the game. Coach Patmon had been notified by district officials and had been asked: "Do you want us to fix it?"

"Leave it," he said. "Maybe it will make us play better."

Nelson Field was filled to near capacity; it was difficult to find a place to park. Folks in Austin call this game the East Side Super Bowl. *Texas Monthly*, a well known magazine had rated the rivalry one of the top eight classics at the high school level. I remember spotting Orlando Hernandez in the crowd during pregame. Orlando was a senior tailback/defensive back at Austin High who I had coached the previous three seasons; I had really enjoyed coaching him. We chatted briefly, I remember enjoying the moment.

The Jaguars may have been 0-4 but they were fired up and ready to play. Both teams traded scores all night, and with less than two minutes we trailed, and it was 3rd down and 17 yards to go. I thought, *we are going to lose.*

LBJ was led by senior defensive back Chris Houston, who would star at the University of Tennessee and play in the NFL for the Atlanta Falcons. For some odd reason, our wide receiver, Anthony Cavanaugh, was able to talk enough 'smack' to convince Chris to come up and play bump and run against him. Cavanaugh was able to get behind him, and we were able to convert the fade into a huge gain. Houston dragged Cavanaugh down at the six yard line. We scored the next play on a dazzling run by Jerrod Williams. We had won.

I remember as we walked across the street back to school, feeling that we were very lucky, and that coaching had little to do with the win. Sometimes the team with better players finds a way to win. Sometimes in spite of poor coaching. Two seasons later I would become friends with LBJ head coach, David Seaborne, and we talked about that 3rd and 17 play.

"I was as baffled as anyone," Coach Seaborne said. "We had a soft zone coverage called, and Chris just did his own thing. It's a shame too because he was a great kid and great player."

Little did I know that Coach Seaborne would essentially be taking my job at Austin Travis in the spring of 2005.

The following week we played Austin McCallum. The Knights played us hard but we ultimately won a very workmanlike game by a final score of 28-7. It set up a showdown with Austin Anderson for the District championship. Anderson was 6-0, (2-0) in District. They were a good team, and had a very explosive offense led by future Stanford product Kyle Gunderson. We were 4-2 (2-0).

The game was played at House Park.

I can't quite describe it, but I knew this game was going to be very special. What I didn't know is that the game would be a roller coaster ride of lead changes and emotions. My father was in attendance so the game already had that much more meaning to me. My father had only attended two games that I had coached and I wanted to prove to him that I was worthy of the viewing. I hoped I passed the audition. I'd be lying if I said I didn't feel a little bit of extra pressure.

Gunderson and the Trojans jumped out to a quick 14-0 lead, the defense slowly made its way to our bench. We needed to meet and make some adjustments.

"Hey, Ben!"

I looked up and saw my father; he was leaning over the railing, trying to get my attention.

"I just wanted to wish you good luck," he said. "Looks like you might be shaving tonight!"

"Thanks Dad, I'll talk to you after the game," I said.

I wasn't amused by his attempt at humor. I knew he was just trying to be funny, but at the moment I didn't appreciate it.

After a few words (with the defensive players) about alignment and defensive responsibilities, I joined the rest of the team on the sideline to watch our offense.

After two consecutive false starts it was 1st and 20. A thirty-five yard post play from quarterback Damien Meyers to Anthony Cavanaugh kept the drive alive. We started to have success running the fly sweep. The fly sweep is an offensive play that the wide receiver, who comes in motion, running at full speed, is given the football. We used it as a way to get to the edge and attack the perimeter, gaining good yardage and utilizing our speed. Often, teams would overcompensate for the fly sweep, opening good running lanes in the middle of the formation. Mixing the belly option and the fly sweep, we scored touchdowns on four consecutive drives to close out the first half with a 28-21 advantage. It had been a shoot-out;forty-nine points were scored in the first half.

Our offense continued to roll and scored twice more to give us a 41-21 lead with 10:09 to play.

The game was far from over.

Anderson caught fire as Gunderson completed a 28 yard touchdown pass to wide receiver B.J. Steele. For some reason, the Trojans attempted a two-point conversion. Perhaps they tried it because we didn't expect it. I know I was caught off guard when I looked up and saw that they were going to run a play. The play went nowhere as Gunderson was immediately pressured and had to throw the football out of bounds. I thought it was premature, but I was glad that they had tried it. It would wind up being a big play in the ball game.

Anderson teed the football up and executed a perfect onside kick. Three plays later they scored a touchdown on a play action post. A play action post is a passing play that when snapped looks like a running play. The play action looks like a run and often gets the safeties to think run, allowing the wide receiver to get behind them. After a successful PAT the score was 41-34 with 4:34 to play.

Our sideline was numb; we had lost all momentum and clung to a seven point lead.

The Anderson place kicker drilled the kickoff out of the end zone. We would start at our own twenty yard line.

Defensive back/wide receiver Roderick Mosely fumbled the football as we attempted to run the fly sweep one more time. We had run it over and over, gaining good yardage all night. For whatever reason, the Anderson defense had failed to make an adjustment to it. But that meant little now; they had the ball inside our twenty yard line and immediately went to the air with the sudden change of possession.

"Touchdown Trojans," an excited game announcer said over the stadium's P.A. system.

Damn it, I thought. *We need something good to happen.* Luckily, that good was going to come on the next play.

Cornerback Cory Sterling timed Anderson's PAT perfectly and blocked it. We held a 41-40 lead with 4:10 remaining on the clock. Anderson kicked it deep. After converting one first down and melting precious time away, we faced 4th and 1 from our own 34 yard line. 1:56 glowed an ominous yellow from the House Park scoreboard.

Coach Patmon called timeout to think it over.

He had decided to go for it. If we failed to pick up the first down Anderson only had to pick up about ten yards to be in field goal range. It was a huge gamble. I wanted to punt it, but I understood why Todd didn't want to. We hadn't really stopped them, and they had all of the game's momentum.

As the play was getting ready to be snapped I thought to myself, *Todd, you have big balls.*

Our fullback was met at the line of scrimmage and appeared to be stopped, but somehow, he managed to spin off the would be tackler and fall forward for four more yards. He was not going to be denied.

We had won. For all intent and purposes we had just won the District championship.

I was elated, and was glad to have won. The defense had played poorly, and I was extremely thankful that the offense had such a tremendous night.

I didn't savor the win like I probably should have. I was young, and in my mind winner's win and loser's lose. And I considered myself a winner.

I still had a lot to learn about life.

Although there were three games left on our schedule, we had little doubt that we would win out and win the district championship. Our next three opponents were having losing seasons, but we prepared for each opponent and left little to chance.

Austin Travis was our next opponent. The Rebels were clearly intimidated in pre-game. If you could score points in pre-game we would have led 50-0.

It was cold and had rained much of the day, the natural grass surface at Burger Center was not in very good playing condition, and it was a fitting arena for our game. We played sloppily, but it didn't matter, we cruised to an easy victory; final score Raiders 47—Rebels 0. Our nose guard Terrell Reese highlighted the game best by stripping the ball from the tailback not once, but twice in the backfield and racing into the end zone for touchdowns on both plays.

The following week we played the Austin Lanier Vikings. It was very similar to the Lockhart game; the Vikings clearly didn't have very athletic players. They were all very skinny and short.They were physically overmatched. But this score would be much uglier, Raiders 63—Vikings 6.

We finished the regular season with a 71-8 victory over Austin Johnston. It was as one sided as the score suggests. It could have been 100-0 if the starters had not been pulled for subs. It was official; we were the 26-4A District champions. Class 4A is any school that has more than 940 students but less than 2,084.

District 26 consists of: Austin Reagan, Austin LBJ, Austin Anderson, Austin Travis, Austin Johnston, Austin Lanier, and Austin McCallum.

It was pretty cool. Our sideline buzzed with excitement. Broad smiles and teeth were highly visible on our side of the field. Goofy grins were everywhere. I was very happy and thrilled for the kids. They had worked hard and been through physically grueling practices. Tee shirts with Reagan Raiders 2002 District champs were being passed out and given to the kids. As the final seconds of the game clock ticked away, our 'twelve piece band' played P. Diddy's *'Bad boy for life.'*

We called the Reagan band a twelve piece because after grades came out, we only had about twelve or so students left who were still eligible to participate in UIL competition. In the state of Texas we have a state law; it is often referred to as 'No Pass, No Play.' If you didn't pass all of your classes, you could not participate in extracurricular activities.

It was a thrilling and neat moment, the kids were all singing the lyrics "we aint going nowhere, we aint going nowhere." We had finished the regular season 8-2, and had developed a bit of a swagger.

"What time is it?" Assistant coach Byron Holmes shouted in a loud booming voice.

"Its playoff time," shouted the Reagan Raider football team.

"What?" Coach Holmes yelled.

"Sheeeiit . . . its playoff time," shouted the football team as they began their pre-game team stretch.

At first glance, Byron Holmes looked intimidating. He was six foot-four, and weighed close to 280 pounds. He was not fat, actually quite lean for someone his size. He had a loud voice. We had become friends; he was a good guy and an excellent football coach. Byron had once been a Parade All-American high school player at Odessa Permian high school. He had played college football at the University of Georgia. We were fortunate to have him.

"We're here to win," Coach Holmes said. "We're here to win. It's playoff time." He continued to repeat the phrase while our boys stretched.

I was hoping the third time was a charm. In my two previous trips to the playoffs, I had been sent home in the first round. I thought, *maybe this could be the year?*

As our boys stretched, I scanned the field. The field's surface was not in very good shape. The grass had more or less abandoned its green, for a brownish-yellow color. White sand filled the many holes in the worn-out grass. Del Valle's Cardinal Stadium had seen better days.

Coach Patmon had decided to flip for the right to play at home at Nelson Field, located directly across the street from Reagan High School. We lost the coin flip; we would play at Del Valle. A coin flip is often used to determine who gets home field advantage in playoff games if the game is not played at a neutral site.

During pre-game, Todd shared with me that one of the assistant principals had asked him to not start our quarterback Damien Meyers. Apparently he had acted up in one of his classes and was very disrespectful towards a teacher.

"What would you do?" Coach Patmon said.

I expressed that we play him, try to get the win, and discipline him later; we had the whole week to assign him punishment if we won. If we lost, then we all lost. Plus, we really hadn't given many practice snaps to our backup quarterback, Brian Ware, who was now sharing time at defensive tackle. Coach Patmon decided to start Damien.

Del Valle gave us everything they had for the first half. We led 3-0 with less than twenty seconds left in the second quarter; we took a knee and jogged it into the visitors' locker room.

As we met to make our halftime adjustments, I mentioned to Coach Patmon that Del Valle had more or less abandoned any formation variations. They were simply running the dive out of double slot. I felt that if we blitzed and played 0 coverage that they couldn't block us and would never expect it.

"What do you want to run?" Coach Patmon said.

"I want to run '*Check Double Psycho Cover 0*'." I said.

"We're playing pretty good defense right now," Coach Patmon said.

"I know Coach, but they have not seen *Check* on film, they don't know that we can run a 3-4." I said. "I think we can catch them off guard and maybe create some turnovers."

"Draw it up," Coach Patmon said.

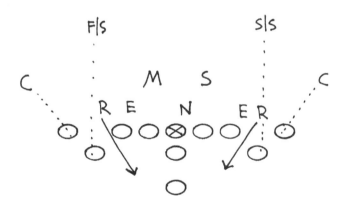

CHECK DOUBLE PSYCHO COVER ZERO

Zero coverage is when a defensive player, almost always a defensive back, is assigned to defend and follow a single offensive player.

"Del Valle has made little effort to establish any type of a passing attack. If they do attempt a bootleg pass of any sort, we will hit the quarterback in the mouth before he has a chance to get the ball off," I explained to Coach Patmon.

In order for us to blitz both perimeter defensive backs we would have to jump back into our 3-4 defensive package. We hadn't really run it in a ball game since our opening loss to Burnet, so it was a risk. We decided it was worth the risk. Del Valle didn't know what had hit them. Before they realized what was going on, our defense had wreaked havoc and the game was essentially over. Del Valle would kick a late field goal and the final score would be 29-3. We were Bi-District champions.

The music was booming, and the kids were having a good time as they dressed and gathered their belongings. Coach Patmon came into the dressing room, he looked down and distraught.

"Are you okay, what's wrong?" I said.

He looked at me than softly said, "You may have to run things for me, I've been suspended from coaching the playoff game next week. There was a miscommunication between me and the administration. Apparently I wasn't supposed to play Damien."

He looked ill; I could see tears swelling in his eyes. We didn't speak any more about it until we met as a staff the following morning.

We would play Fredericksburg in the area championship the following week. Once again we lost the coin flip; we would have to play Fredericksburg at Fredericksburg.

Fredericksburg is a small predominantly German town located in the hill country about eighty miles from Austin.

They had great fans. It was loud, and it was a sea of red, the home team's colors. The overflow bleachers were already full as we went out for pregame stretch.

The Reagan administration decided that Coach Patmon could coach the second half of the playoff game, but he would be relegated to the press box for the first half.

Just moments before kickoff, District 26-4A Defensive MVP, nose guard Terrell Reese was pacing the sidelines, fuming with anger and talking to himself.

I had Terrell in my United States history class so I had developed a pretty good relationship with him, occasionally driving him home after football practice.

I went over to Terrell and put my arm around him.

He was a rock; his body was chiseled from hours of weight lifting.

"What's wrong?" I said.

I looked in his eyes, I saw sheer terror. Terrell handed me his helmet.

"There are spiders in my helmet Coach," Terrell said.

It was clear to me that he had not taken his medication for a while.

Not missing a beat, I inspected his helmet. I grabbed a water bottle and gave it a squirt. I pretended to scoop out the spiders. I gave the helmet back to Terrell.

"I got them all out," I said.

"Thanks Coach," said Terrell, looking relieved and a bit more relaxed.

Then he went out and did what he does, draw double teams.

The Battlin' Billies gave us all we could handle. They had a big, physical offensive line which gave us problems all night. But ultimately, we made a few more big plays than they did. We left Fredericksburg with a thrilling 39-28 victory.

"Where is Jerrod Williams?" Coach Patmon barked.

Williams and several other players had missed practice for an assortment of reasons. We did not have a good week of work. Although school was not in session due to the Thanksgiving holidays, football practice was supposed to be in full swing.

Our ten game winning streak and playoff run came to a screeching halt with a 42-14 loss to Gregory-Portland at the Alamodome.

I had been outcoached and our kids had been outplayed. Our season was over.

In a way, I felt some relief. I was physically and mentally drained.

The following morning I was forced to shave my scraggly bird-nest of a beard.

A tear ran down my cheek as I turned my electric razor on.

Seven Ellis, Ben Jacobs, and Brit Navarro pose for a picture moments after a character education class.

Quarterback Sean Alonzo looks for a wide receiver to come open.

Ben Jacobs and Gene Scoggins take time to take a picture after the conclusion of a Boyz into Men meeting.

Ben Jacobs lectures during a Boyz into Men lesson.

The 2011 Roosevelt Rough Riders.

Ben Jacobs and defensive back Brit Navarro
make adjustments on the sideline.

Ben Jacobs and defensive back Sedric
Wolford discuss defensive coverages.

The 2011 Roosevelt football team stands united.

Chapter 15

2003

The next school day (Monday, March 31) after her daughter's murder, Loretta Daniels addressed our student body over the school's P.A. system.

"Eve is fine. She loves you all," she said. "She knows you love her."

After the murder of Eve Daniels on school grounds I just wasn't sure if Reagan was a place that I wanted to stay for an extended period of time. I had a really good job offer (coaching football and baseball) from Round Rock high school but turned it down because I didn't want to lose my title as defensive coordinator. Being a defensive coordinator was fun, and I really didn't want to return to being an assistant coach. I wanted to be a head football coach someday, and I felt like the coordinator's title was something that I needed to help me achieve my goal.

2003 was one of my least enjoyable seasons. We were coming off a 10-3 season, and expectations were high; but we were simply not as good.

We were blown out in our opener to Burnet 47-0. Stephen McGee and Jordan Shipley torched us all night. I can honestly say that I have never seen a duo like them before, and may never again. The loss was embarrassing.

The following week we were totally humiliated. We lost to Leander 78-18. We had quit playing and looked like we hadn't ever been coached. I remember walking back across the street to Reagan from the stadium after the game, thinking I was going to be shot.

Everybody dressed quickly and attempted to leave. Coach Patmon wasn't as fortunate, an angry parent cussed him profusely just outside of our field house.

It would be a long night, after the fireworks were done; we met and discussed the possibility that we might have a very difficult job ahead of us.

We weren't very talented, and we had even less character. There was work to be done.

We played very hard the next week. Playing hard does not always mean you play well. We lost a heart breaker, 3-0 to Lampassas. I remember as we loaded the bus I was able to tell Coach Patmon that I was encouraged. Although we lost, I saw many positives. We were 0-3, and written off by the local media; that suited us just fine. The following week we played Lockhart at Nelson Field. Two weeks earlier we had lost a game by sixty points. This Friday night belonged to us. Although we didn't play terribly well, we played with great effort. We shut out Lockhart 18-0, earning our first win of the season.

The East Side Super Bowl was next: LBJ vs. Reagan.

It was a great game as usual, a real bruiser. We won 14-13.

We were beginning to gel as a team. Our offense was beginning to fire on all cylinders. We won six of our final seven games to qualify for the playoffs. As bad as the season had started, we were only a 14-7 last second loss to Anderson away from being district champions.

We would play New Braunfels Canyon in the first round of the playoffs. We would have to play them at their place, The Cougar Den.

We played extremely hard, but lost a tough 35-18 contest to the Cougars.

While the kids were dressing to go back home, Coach Patmon pulled me aside to talk to me.

"Ben, you should probably start looking. If you can get out you should," Coach Patmon said. "This place (Reagan) is going downhill in a hurry."

I didn't know how to take his words at the time, looking back now in retrospect I think Coach Patmon was trying to help me.

I took his advice. My days as a Reagan Raider were over. Coach Patmon was right; Reagan has not won more than two games in a football season to date. It would also become an academically low performing school. Austin ISD officials debated closing Reagan High School due to low standardized test scores and high absenteeism. Reagan High School currently remains open, although student enrollment has continued to decline.

Chapter 16

TR

TURNING

BOYZ

Into

MEN

January 11th

Tuesday, 8 A.M.

TEAM Room

Invest in yourself

Something happened after the conclusion of our first ever Turning Boyz into Men meeting. Roosevelt football players were talking about character, accepting responsibility and false masculinity.

"Are you going to have another meeting next week Coach," a freshmen football player asked me.

"Yes I am, every Tuesday at 8am," I said. "I'd love to have you."

Word of mouth had spread like a wild fire. We had more football players at our next meeting. We also had another coach who wanted to help with our meetings. Gene Scoggins, our defensive line coach wanted to be a part of our meeting. We welcomed him with open arms.

"Why are we here?" I asked the players.

"To be a better man," the players shouted back.

"What?" I said.

"To be a better man," the players shouted louder.

"What is your job?" I asked.

"To love each other," the boys replied.

"I can't hear you," I said.

"To love each other," the boys roared back.

Before beginning our two discussion questions, we reviewed our four rules. These four rules would serve as our guide to becoming better men. A question was once again visible courtesy of the projector.

HE ACCEPTS RESPONSIBILTY

(Discussion)

What does this look like?

The boys exchanged answers and opinions. As a group we decided that waking up early, going to all your classes on time, and showing up to practice were good starting points.

"We all have problems," I said. "It's how you respond. Rich people, poor people, all people hurt and have wounds. How are you going to address those wounds? Hopefully, it doesn't take you as long as it took me to accept responsibility."

After some serious discussion, it was evident to me that they had a pretty good grasp of what accepting responsibility looked like.

Next, we addressed our 2nd rule: HE LEADS COURAGEOUSLY.

I could not use biblical references so I used real people as examples of leading others with courage. I mentioned Tom Landry and Martin Luther King.

Nelson Mandela, Cesar Chavez, and Jackie Robinson were just a few of the examples that the kids brought up. We discussed why they were great leaders.

"What does leading with courage look like to you?" I asked the group.

"It is someone who isn't afraid to do the right thing," Christian Pastrano said. "He is someone who isn't worried about what others might think about him."

"Great answer," I said. "Anyone else?"

"I think being a leader takes courage because you have to be willing to be different, to set yourself apart from the rest," Sean Alonzo said. "Some days you will get a lot of the credit, others you will get most of the blame."

"Spoken like a quarterback," I said.

Sean smiled and rubbed the dark peach fuzz that was growing on his chin.

HE LEADS COURAGEOUSLY

The second of our four rules.

I thought, *just because you tell kids that you have to lead, that doesn't mean that it's going to happen. Kids have to be shown how to lead, actually put into positions and situations to lead.*

I decided I was going to make it my mission to try to mold a few young men into leaders.

On January 11 we started a tradition of handing out two awards each meeting. Our Quarterback Sean Alonzo and Free Safety Leland Young were the first two award winners for exhibiting outstanding leadership during the 2010 football season. Each player was given a certificate that I had gotten all of our coaching staff to sign.

Both Sean and Leland were great players, 1ˢᵗ team 26-5A all-district players to be exact. But they were also outstanding young men; I was honored to have coached them.

I had them stand in front of their peers while I bragged about them.

While praising these two young men in front of their peers, I made it clear how I felt about them. Although they were seniors, and would be graduating, it was not the end of our relationship. In many ways it was actually just the beginning. I can't wait to see what kind of men they will become. I'm anxious to know them long into their adult years.

Leland Young is one of those rare young men that if you ever get a chance to coach, you cherish the opportunity. I never heard a complaint or anything negative come out of his mouth in the four years that I coached him. He always went through every drill, every practice at full speed. During the 2010 Thanksgiving holidays, just a week after we had been eliminated from the playoffs, I picked up my cell phone and called Leonard Young, Leland's father.

"I just wanted you to know how much I enjoyed coaching your son," I said. "I think he is a terrific kid. You and your wife did a great job of raising Leland. I'm proud to have coached him. Whatever you'll did at home, it worked."

"Well thank you Coach, but I can't take too much of the credit," Mr. Young said. "Leland is a low maintenance kid. You don't really have to do a lot for him. He knows what he has to do and he does it. But to tell you the truth Coach, I want to thank you. Leland had a great experience playing football at Roosevelt. Leland appreciated the fact that you didn't have to yell to get your point across. He enjoyed being a defensive back and being coached by you. He respects you. You were fair and consistent. That meant a lot to Leland."

I was near tears by the time I had hung up the phone with Leland's father. I was going to miss coaching him. I was saddened that he could not play anymore football for Roosevelt High School.

After the meeting had ended I walked back to the coaches' office with Coach Scoggins. I was still kind of walking on air as I got to my desk.I took a deep breath and took a seat. I had a buzzing sensation and I felt good, I felt that I was making a difference in kids' lives.

"That went well," Coach Scoggins said.

"I thought so," I said. "Do you think the team room is too big to hold our meetings in?"

"If you want a smaller room you can use my class room," Coach Scoggins said.

"Thanks Gene, I think that would make our lessons a little more intimate, kind of force the kids to get out of their comfort zone," I said.

"Do you need me to do anything? What can I do to help?" Coach Scoggins said.

"You're doing it already, thanks man,"' I said.

Coach Scoggins smiled at me and patted me on the back. Then he grabbed his things and was off to teach his first period world history class. I didn't have a class first period so I often got some much needed alone time to reflect on life or prepare for my classes that soon enough I would be upstairs in; knee deep in Algebra.

I looked at my desk and admired the many pictures of my children that were present and proudly displayed.

I was a lucky man.

I hadn't always felt that way. I zoned out for a few minutes, my thoughts drifting back to the odd circumstances that led me to Roosevelt. It had been an icky, pride swallowing siege; one that I was in a way, ashamed of. Actually, the whole hiring process and then my first year at Roosevelt in general had been surrounded in personal turmoil and anguish for me. I had often thought, *God, why am I here?*

I knew why now. It was an opportunity to help others.

Chapter 17

It's always amazed me how tough it was to find a job coaching somewhere that you truly wanted to be. I was a new father and still somewhat of a new husband. Although I had not been fired, there was no way I was going to accept a demotion at Travis High School.

I had been a coordinator for the past three seasons and really didn't want to be an assistant any more. The new head coach at Austin Reagan was an old friend of mine, Paul Darby, Sr.

Paul was a well built light skinned African-American man with a very warm and mild temperament. Paul had also played pro football for the New York Jets. We had coached together, and I liked him. I was also lucky enough to have coached his son.

We discussed me returning to Reagan and after much contemplating I had made a decision. I was going to return to Reagan as offensive coordinator. But I guess God had other plans for me.

The brand new Reagan principal, John Rodriguez wasn't really convinced that I wanted to be at Reagan. We had already interviewed once, but he wanted to meet again, away from school grounds. We made arrangements to meet and talk at a south Austin Starbucks.

After chatting for about thirty minutes, he was sold on the idea of me returning to Reagan.

But, Reagan was a low performing school and the director of the Reagan campus, who was also in charge of the principal, was really slowing things down.

Dr. Bert Jones apparently wanted to 'see me sweat it out.' I called and called to see why the transfer had not yet been approved. Coach Darby told me try to be patient and wait it out.

"It's going to happen; he (Dr. Jones) just wants to see you sweat a little bit," Coach Darby said. "Try to be patient."

I grew tired of waiting; I just didn't trust Dr. Jones. I was growing terribly impatient.

I remembered my days at Austin High, and thought about how competitive we were, and yet we got crushed in the playoffs by our first round opponents from North East ISD in San Antonio for two consecutive seasons.

It was then I thought if you want to be the best, go and learn what they do. I had a plan. I went with my gut. I got on the telephone and made an appointment. Next, I interviewed with North East ISD Athletic Director Jerry Comalander.

Coach Comalander was somewhat of a living legend around the San Antonio area. He had coached for many years, and was the head football coach when San Antonio Churchill won its one and only State Championship. I was terribly nervous, not everybody has a stadium named after themselves, especially while they are still living.

We talked a lot, mostly football stuff, which I really enjoyed; I liked him almost instantly. I could see that he was kid oriented, and that he truly wanted what was best for kids.

But there was a problem; there were no coaching openings in the district at the present time. Then he explained that were seldom any openings in football.

"North East is a tough place to get your foot in the door," Coach Comalander said. "It's a good district, and we pay pretty well too."

"I'll do whatever it takes," I said. I wanted the chance to coach in North East and see what I could do.

Coach Comalander was honest and fair with me. "Let me make a few phone calls and see what I can do," he said. We shook hands and I left his office. I made it to the parking lot where I found my car. It was hot and I badly wanted to take off my black over-sized sport coat. It was time to go home.

The following week I received a phone call from Head Coach Glenn Hightower at San Antonio Roosevelt. He wanted to see if I could drive down to San Antonio and come in for an interview. I drove down to see him the very same day.

We hit it off right away. I was very impressed with him. He quizzed me about various places I had been and defensive schemes I had run as a coordinator. He wanted to know what defense we ran when I was an assistant at Austin High.

"We were mostly a 4-2-5 defense based out of cover 3," I said.

Cover 3 is a defense that assigns both cornerbacks and the free safety to each cover the deep one-third of the field. They are each responsible for anyone who comes into their area.

"Why did you'll run that; that's like pulling up your skirt," Coach Hightower said, politely laughing as he scribbled something on a note pad that lay on his desk.

I wanted to work for him right then.

"I agree," I said. "You do give up a lot of things when you play cover three. It is definitely a bend but don't break defense."

I glanced up and looked at the numerous golden football trophies that were just above his head, displayed on a shiny mahogany-like wooden shelf.

Coach Hightower had a great knowledge of football and I enjoyed talking with him.

"You are going to have to be a volunteer football coach," Coach Hightower said. "I don't really have anything available, but I can probably get you a spring sport stipend. You might have to coach soccer."

"I have also been offered the offensive coordinator position at Austin Reagan," I said. "I will have to talk with Coach Darby before I make a decision."

He smiled and said, "Well, I know what I would do."

On my drive home I called my friend David Hoff, who was now the head coach at Red Water High School. I explained to him my dilemma. He listened, and then proceeded with an answer. "If you have the chance to work for Coach Hightower, you should take it." Coach Hoff said. "He (Coach Hightower) knows football, and he does it the right way."

I had made my decision; I was going to San Antonio Roosevelt. I wanted to be a Rough Rider.

Little did I know that actually getting hired was going to be a very stressful ordeal. Shortly after letting Coach Hightower know that I was on board, I received a phone call from him.

"I can't hire you, something has come up on your criminal history report that was a red flag," Coach Hightower said. "Is there anything you need to tell me about?"

"Well, I guess so," I said, wiping my forehead as sweat began to accumulate. "I had been arrested for DWI in 2000 but that charge had long since been dropped. In college I had gotten into a fight, but that too had been dismissed, it was ancient history. I have been teaching and coaching for the past seven years." I was dumbfounded how it might be a problem now.

Coach Hightower paused, as if not knowing what to say, he cleared his throat.

"I can't hire you," Coach Hightower said. "You better find a way to fix it."

I made an appointment with the principal, William Lewis, who had agreed to see me.

I was embarrassed. I didn't know how to tell him, *I'm here to get a job, and by the way, I've been told that you can't hire me because I've been arrested twice, although all charges were dismissed.*

I decided that I wouldn't sugar coat it, I was very matter of fact and told him what had happened. I figured that there was nothing he could do anyway.

"Ben, try to relax," Mr. Lewis said. "You are a different person than the one you were in college. I believe everyone deserves a second chance, don't you?"

"I do," I said. "That was a long time ago, when I was quite young and immature."

"We all have done things that we regret," Mr. Lewis said compassionately. "We all have done foolish things when we were young."

I could tell from the look in his eyes that he was sincere and not just blowing smoke.

I showed him my court documents and proof that all charges had been dismissed. He got on the phone and called James Salazar, who was in charge of hiring new teachers.

Once again I had to explain that when I was in college I made some poor choices and had gotten into a fight out of self-defense. He (Mr. Salazar) showed me his computer screen where it read that the charge against me was still pending. I showed him my court papers; he agreed that the charges had indeed been dropped.

At the end of the day, I had a job. *What a way to get hired,* I thought.

I was ashamed and felt like a criminal, but there was really no one else to blame but myself.

On the drive back to Austin I became terribly ill. My vision was blurry and my stomach felt very uneven. I had to pull over and vomit. I didn't know it yet, but I just had my first official migraine. Eventually I made it home; I walked in the door, hugged my wife, and ran to the toilet. I was sick again, I just didn't quite know why.

The 2005 season was just as crazy as the hiring process I had just encountered.

I didn't know a soul in San Antonio when I began coaching at Roosevelt. It was a period of great adjustment for me. My ego took a huge beating. I tried my best to handle the fact that I voluntarily agreed to accept a job that meant I would not be getting paid a stipend for coaching football. I was not used to being the low man on the totem pole. Long time coaching veteran Jeff Hooks welcomed me and made me feel right at home. He was a good coach, and a better man. He had a wealth of knowledge. He had coached for twenty-seven years, including twelve as a head coach.

Coach Hooks is one of the hardest working men I have ever known. I worked hard, and I was almost always at work by seven o'clock. The school day did not start until nine o'clock but I always made sure that I was adequately prepared for each day.Coach Hooks was always already at work when I arrived, usually passing out laundry. Most days he was jamming out to music as he stuffed the laundry into individual players' lockers. We quickly became friends, and laundry partners.

Passing out the laundry everyday with someone really gives you an opportunity to get to know that person. Coach Hooks and I often exchanged stories about places we had coached. Some of our stories were humorous, and others were simply hard to believe. But they were all real.

"Roosevelt is just a different place, it's different from anywhere else that I have been," Coach Hooks said. "I have coached for a long time, and I've seen some things. One night after a game I was driving one of our players home. He lived in the Glen, and apparently you don't go to the Glen at night."

The Glen is a neighborhood that many of our football players and members of our student body live. "I got stopped as I pulled into the entrance of his street, and it wasn't by the police." Coach Hooks said. "These guys all dressed in red jump suits wanted to see my driver's license. I was about to show it to them when the kid I was driving home spoke up."

"No, no, no," the young man said. "He's cool, he's my coach."

"Anyway. They let me drop the kid off," Coach Hooks said. "As I pulled out of the neighborhood, let's just say I was glad to be leaving. I was a little nervous. I kept checking the rear view mirror my whole way home. My four years at Roosevelt really aged me."

Working at a challenging school didn't really bother me. But his story did make me pause and think, *I might be back at Austin Reagan. No, more like Denzel Washington's Training Day.*

I helped Coach Hooks coach the defensive backs. Mostly I handled aspects of our weekly scouting reports. During the practice week I was in charge of running the scout team. The scout team is a team that consists of eleven players, it also serves as the group of men that try and imitate your opponent. Our defense punished the scout team. We were fast and physical. We felt that we had a chance to have a pretty good defensive football team.

We beat up East Central High School 31-10 in our season opener.

The following week we played Samuel Clemens and highly touted tailback and University of Texas commitment James Henry. We played well defensively but lost a hard fought 15-3 battle. We were 1-1.

We responded with a blow out win. We smothered Corpus Christi King 42-0. We dominated, limiting King's offense to a total of thirty-five yards.

We opened district play with a thrilling 19-17 last second come from behind win over San Antonio Churchill. We were 3-1 and beginning to gel as a team.

Then, with seemingly no hint at all that it was coming, the rug was taken out from beneath our feet. Two days before our show down with San Antonio Madison, we had received news that four of our best players were being suspended for the remainder of the season.

Apparently that summer, right before I had been hired, four Roosevelt football players had taken some computers from the school. When Mr. Lewis found out about it, he called the boys that he had heard were responsible for the theft. All stolen computer equipment was returned to the school. The players were punished, assigned a summer assignment, and made to serve countless hours of community service.

Well apparently, that wasn't good enough.

Allegedly, Mr. Lewis, rather than call the police, dealt with the problem internally and the boys served their punishment. Rather than get the police involved in what might have been a criminal matter, he handled it.

I think what he did was admirable, but apparently the local media did not. It was widely viewed that Mr. Lewis didn't go through the proper channels, and that the matter had been swept under the rug; the powers at be felt that athletes had received preferential treatment.

Two days after the boys had been dismissed from the team, Mr. Lewis resigned. This still saddens me to this day. The boys paid a hefty price for their behavior, and one of them lost a scholarship to a Big XII school to play football.

Mr. Lewis had helped me get a job and I will never forget it.

I believe that he was doing what he thought was best for kids.

With many backups forced into starting roles, we simply were not the same team. We gave many good teams all they could handle, and led the eventual state runner-up Converse Judson for a good portion of our game, but we came up short. We finished 4-6. It was the first time in six years I had not been to the playoffs. Shortly after the season had ended, Coach Hightower announced that he was leaving to become the head coach at Conroe Caney Creek.

"All of you are more than welcomed to be a part of my new staff," he said. "Thank you for all of your hard work. I know this year was not easy."

Going to Conroe simply was not an option for me. I was still paying on my vacant and unsold house in Austin and living with my in-laws in San Antonio. I thought to myself, *good times! It sucks to be me.*

Once again I would have to go through the process of waiting for the next head coach to be named.

Chapter 18

"Why are we here?" I asked the players.

"To be a better man," the players shouted back.

"What?" I said.

"To be a better man," the players shouted louder.

"What is your job?" I asked.

"To love each other," the boys replied.

"I can't hear you," I said.

"To love each other," the boys roared back.

I presented our four rules to guide us via the projector, and quickly went over our mission statement. It read:

TR Turning Boyz into Men

Our Mission:

To empower Roosevelt football players to be their best by:

Learning how to love and be loved, and initiating individual positive relationships with team mates and and/or other members of the Roosevelt community.

We had mentioned rules three and four but had not yet really discussed what they were and what they meant.

Our 3rd rule was: HE HELPS OTHERS.

We discussed it for the next ten minutes. The twenty-four boys who were in attendance had a pretty firm understanding of what the rule looked like, and what it meant.

"Do you help others?" I asked.

Only five boys raised their hands. The rule was so simple. Yet, very few people do indeed help others.

"Why don't we help others?" I asked.

"Because it is hard Coach," one of the boys said, responding to the question. "It's almost like you have to plan it. Man, that takes a lot of time."

"It can certainly feel that way at times," I said.

"Why should I help others?" A young man asked.

"Shut up you fool," shouted one of the boys.

"No, no," I said. "It's fine, all questions are welcomed. You ask a good question. I can't talk to you about God, but this is what I think. Take from it what you will. I think you should help others because don't you and I want to be treated well? I know this sounds a bit corny, but I really believe that you have to treat others the way you would want to be treated. It helps foster a sense of community. There is more to this world than just you and me. I try to think about what I would want, and I try to do that for others. It's not always easy."

"Sorry for that long answer," I said. "I hope you got something out of it."

"Now it's time to present our next two award winners," I said. "Tevin Ellis. Come on up here my man, come and get your certificate. It is my pleasure to give this to you."

The week before I had witnessed Tevin helping a learning disabled student in the hallway. He helped others often, whether it was in football or at school; he was just a sweet kid. He grinned momentarily while the other members of the group applauded him. He shook my hand, grabbed his certificate and quickly returned to his seat.

"The next certificate for he helps others goes to, Coach Gene Scoggins," I said.

Gene walked to the front of the class room and shook my hand. Gene was a big man. He was six foot-four, and weighed nearly 340 pounds. He was blushing, and his cheeks were flushed a very rosy red color.

"Thank you Coach," Gene said.

During our last ten minutes we examined our 4th rule: HE DOES THE RIGHT THING.

"We are all born with a sense of right and wrong," I said. "This rule is about your character."

Coach LaHue had talked to our players often about character. 'Character is what you do when no one else is looking' he liked to say. He especially liked to talk about character after a loss.

I used his phrase to try to drive home my point.

"Character is this: what kind of a person are you?" I said.

Our fourth and final rule was so simple, yet very difficult. I used Coach LaHue's phrase to further try to explain.

"What kind of person are you; would you steal if you could get away with it? Would you cheat on a test? Would you cheat on your girlfriend?" I said.

I thanked the kids for showing up and I dismissed them to go to their first period class. I gathered my materials and was closing down my laptop when Coach Scoggins spoke to me.

"Coach, thank you," he said. "I had no clue that you were going to present me with an award. I haven't really done anything."

"Yes, you have," I said. "You are here, and you are supportive of these kids and supportive of me. Thank you, and thanks for letting me use your room. I appreciate your help."

"Speaking of help, I would like to help." Gene said. "What can I do?"

"Umm, do you feel comfortable teaching a lesson like I do it?" I said.

"Sure, Coach," Gene said. "Just tell me what you want it on?"

"Marriage," I said. "I suspect a lot of our kids come from broken homes, and I think you would be the right guy to talk to them about it."

Chapter 19

It was the spring of 2006, and I did not have an official position as a football coach. Roosevelt had named Neal Lahue its new head football coach. He came with impressive credentials; he had won a State championship in 1996 at Austin Westlake, and had been a coordinator at the college level. I thought I could learn some football from him. I quickly tried to sell myself to him.

He basically told me that I was going to have to 'try out', and that he was going to evaluate me. I felt pretty down. Essentially, I had given up a coordinator position to be a volunteer assistant for Coach Hightower. And now, Coach Hightower was long gone. I thought, *I'm screwed; I might have to return to Austin.*

My wife's grandmother lived in the Rio Grande Valley, in a tiny city named Elsa. The Rio Grande Valley is the part of Texas that is south of Corpus Christi. It is the large area of land that lies between the United States and Mexico.

There was a job opening there, less than sixty miles from the Mexican border that intrigued me. The job paid slightly more than I made in San Antonio, and I could stay with Mandy's grandmother for free until our house in Austin sold. I could be a coordinator again, which was something that was important to me.

Los Fresnos High School was looking to hire a defensive coordinator. Los Fresnos was led by Frank Simmons. He was a heck of a head coach and I thought that the job could be a gold mine and maybe help me one day be a head coach. I had watched some Los Fresnos film while preparing to play Gregory-Portland in the regional semi-finals when I was at Austin Reagan.

I phoned Coach Simmons about the opening and we quickly made plans to set up an interview.

I nailed the interview. I had to present my defensive package to Coach Simmons and his defensive staff. I could tell that he liked what I presented. I answered all of his questions. I had prepared clips of game film of the defensive package that I hoped to install.

Coach Simmons and I had lunch together at an old Mexican restaurant. The enchiladas were delicious. The smell of home-made flour tortillas gave the cozy restaurant an inviting aroma.

I could tell from his line of questioning that he was impressed with me.

"If I made you the offer right now, what would you say," Coach Simmons said.

"I would accept," I said.

"I'll be calling you very soon," he said.

He called; it just wasn't the phone call I was expecting. "There was a red flag on your criminal history. Is there anything you need to tell me about?" Coach Simmons said.

I couldn't believe it, not again. I thought, *Déjà vu.*

I located my court documents and faxed him all of my papers two days later. The documents showed and proved that all criminal charges had been dismissed. But it was too late, the damage had been done. He had offered the job to another candidate.

Los Fresnos would go 12-1 the next 2 consecutive seasons.

I fell into somewhat of a depression. I was terribly down, mostly feeling sorry for myself for a few weeks. I thought ,why does this keep happening to me? *I'm a good person, how could one stupid fight from my college days continue to haunt me.*

I phoned Coach Hightower and asked him if there was anything that he could do to help me. He once again asked if I wanted to go to Conroe as an assistant, I appreciated the offer, but I was still living with my in laws and paying a mortgage on my house in Austin.

I needed a job in or around San Antonio. He set up an interview for me with a friend of his who was the head coach at San Antonio O'Connor. I interviewed at O'Connor; it didn't go very well.

Coach Michael Ross had asked me how things were going for me at Roosevelt; I didn't really know what to say.

"I guess things are going okay," I said. "Things are different now. I didn't come to Roosevelt to work for Coach LaHue. I had come there to work for Coach Hightower."

I was probably perceived to be negative, but that was not my intention, I simply tried to answer the questions honestly. At this particular moment in time, I didn't really feel any sense of loyalty to Coach LaHue. He had not yet hired me as an assistant coach and I wanted a paid coaching job.

The next day Coach LaHue called me into his office. He was pretty angry with me, raising his voice often. I had never really had to coach for someone who yelled at me before, and I didn't really plan on starting now.

He was pissed off.

"I don't appreciate you going over there (O'Connor) and bad mouthing me." Coach LaHue said. "That guy (Coach Ross) over there, he's a friend of mine. You showed no loyalty to me. You know, the kids really like you here. But I'll be honest with you. I don't know if I can trust you."

Well, he was right about the loyalty part. But, I did not go badmouth him or anyone else that day. I remember telling him that loyalty is earned, and asking why should I be loyal yet. I didn't even have a paid coaching stipend or a place on his staff. I was pretty angry by this point as well.

Regretfully, I quit coaching, and I did not do it the right way. I had looked for Neal all day, and I could not find him. I felt that it couldn't wait. I wrote him a letter basically stating that I would not be coaching for him. I was not going to 'try out' any more. I was a good coach, but I thought that it was best if I went in another direction.

I half heartedly searched for a few other coaching jobs. I interviewed at Poteet High School for the offensive coordinator position, but after viewing the field house and talking with the head coach, I pulled out of the running for the job. My friend Paul Darby offered me the offensive coordinator position at Austin Reagan again, but there was just no way I was going to make that long commute and not be with my family; I declined the offer.

I called Coach Isaac Martinez at Harlandale about an assistant job, and we set up an interview. But the day before our interview I phoned Coach Martinez and let him know that I wasn't interested. I was feeling sorry for myself in many different ways: professionally, financially, and emotionally.

My career as a coach seemed to be going in the wrong direction. I thought, *why?*

Financially, most of the money we were able to save I had just spent. Our house in Austin had finally sold. I had to write a check for $15,000 to get the deal done. We had lost most of our savings.

My marriage was experiencing problems as well. I was letting hardships from work interfere with my home life. I loved my wife deeply, but something in our relationship seemed to be lacking. I thought, *we aren't great anymore.* I was sad.

I felt the best thing for me and my family at the time was to not coach. I wanted to see if just being a teacher and being around home more would be better for my family.

I was tired of living with my in-laws. The stress caused from the lifestyle adjustment of having to live with Mandy's parents was not helping matters either. We needed a change of scenery.

We purchased a small home in Converse, which is just north east of San Antonio. I was going to focus on being a husband and a father.

I had tons of free time. I just didn't know what to do with myself. As much as I enjoyed being a father and watching Isabella grow up, I was miserable.

I missed high school football; I missed the relationships that I had formed with the football players. I attempted to watch a couple of high school football games as a spectator. It hurt too much; it was actually painful for me to watch. I thought, *I should be on that side line, that should be me.*

I was a coach.

I knew what I had to do.

I had heard that Coach LaHue had several openings on his staff that he needed to fill. I went and found him, and we visited briefly with each other.

He offered me a job. I was thrilled but tried to hide my excitement.

"Now Ben, I need you to know something before you start," Coach LaHue said. "These guys you'll be working with, they are not perfect coaches, but they are my guys. Can you do things my way?"

Chapter 20

"Why are we here?" I asked the players.

"To be a better man," the players shouted back.

"What?" I said.

"To be a better man," the players shouted louder.

"What is your job?" I asked.

"To love each other," the boys replied.

"I can't hear you," I said.

"To love each other," the boys roared back.

I thanked the boys for coming. Orange juice and donuts had been provided, a few of the boys snacked while they continued to write.

As a warm up I had our boys complete a hand out. It was lying on their desks as they came into the classroom.

TR TURNING BOYZ INTO MEN

Name **Christian Pastrano**

Date **2/1/2011**

What do you hope to accomplish from our meetings?

To become a better man

What is one thing that I should know about you?

I haven't seen my biological dad since age 11. He used to abuse my mom. I have a step dad named Mike. He's the greatest thing that has ever happened to me. My biological dad leaving out of my life had made me stronger—how to be on my own.

What was the best day of your life, so far?

When my dad left and my step dad came into my life.

I read each player's handout while we watched a short video clip from former San Antonio Spur David Robinson.

I was amazed at their responses, the boys had written many powerful tidbits about themselves. I thought, *many of these boys are truly amazing people.*

The kids really got into the video. There was this hall of fame basketball player, whose body and arms were chiseled like an oak tree telling us that money, sex, and fame had nothing to do with being a real man. 'I'm a dad. I'm a husband; I'm a Man . . . who just happens to be a pretty good basket ball player.'

The kids were floored; they heard it from me all the time, but coming from the mouth of David Robinson was something else entirely.

I thought, *what a great man he is. Thank you David.*

I knew that most of the kids in the group felt that they were just an ordinary person, trying to find a niche in this world. I knew that I often felt that way. I had something to say to them.

"I am just an ordinary man," I said. "All of us, as individuals are just ordinary. But as a whole, as a team, we have the ability to become extraordinary. You should love being part of a team. What we have, not everyone gets to have this."

Chapter 21

The 2007 season seemed doomed right from the start. In what I was told was an oversight, Coach LaHue had forgotten to notify me about our first staff meeting. I thought, *that's not good. That's not a good sign. These guys are going to think I'm a slacker.* And I was far from that.

We made a commitment to 'go young.' We were going to have to play a lot of sophomores. Officially I was the wide receivers coach, but I was basically Coach Anthony Boykin's assistant. Anthony was our co-offensive coordinator, but he really was in charge of the wide receivers. I learned a lot from him; I can truly say that he is the best wide receivers coach I've ever been around. He would also become one of my dear friends.

We finished the season 5-5. Quite frankly, I felt that we overachieved. We were not a very talented football team, but still found a way to finish with a .500 record.

We finished one win away from a possible playoff berth. In order to advance to the playoffs we would have had to defeat San Antonio Reagan. The Reagan Rattlers were led by San Antonio's leading rusher and Georgia Tech bound Marcus Wright. We led 7-0 early, but as all great backs do, Wright wiggled free for two long runs and we lost 17-7.

We pride ourselves that we play high school football in the state of Texas. Texas is widely regarded as one of the best, most competitive states in regards to high school football. And despite the fact that we were young and not very good, we played toe to toe with the best our district had to offer. District 26-5A consisted of: Converse Judson, Converse Wagner, Smithson Valley, San Antonio Roosevelt, San Antonio Churchill, San Antonio Madison, San Antonio, MacArthur, San Antonio Reagan, and San Antonio Lee. Our schedule was brutal; we played a great opponent every week. District 26-5A in many circles is regarded as the best in the state, so therefore we play against and with the nation's best football teams.

I was the head coach of the 9th grade B team, and I wanted to show everyone that I was a great coach and why I was once a coordinator. I coached the freshmen the way I did the varsity when I was a coordinator. I scripted our call sheet, and Ischemed each opponent. We went 10-0.

Coaching with a chip on your shoulder might be effective from a wins and losses perspective, but it is not very enjoyable or fulfilling. Looking back in retrospect, we were good because we had good players. Players make plays, and they certainly did. Led by Leland Young and Joshua Glass, we dominated our opponents. Despite the many wins on the football field, I felt empty. I felt like I always had to prove myself; I was not comfortable in my own skin. I felt like a feather floating aimlessly. In many ways, I felt like a nobody.

Chapter 22

"Why are we here?" I asked the players.

"To be a better man," the players shouted back.

"What?" I said.

"To be a better man," the players shouted louder.

"What is your job?" I asked.

"To love each other," the boys replied.

"I can't hear you," I said.

"To love each other," the boys roared back.

Like we do every meeting, we quickly reviewed our four rules to guide us and our mission statement.

Today we were going to tackle a new subject.

Treatment of women.

I was concerned that many of our boys, society in general, didn't place much value on women.

I felt that all too often, men only see women in terms of sex. I was also concerned that we didn't know how to appreciate women. We didn't know what we wanted out of a partner.

I thought it was an important part of being a man; knowing how to love a woman.

"How can you have a good relationship if you don't feel women have any value," I said.

I heard one young man quietly snicker and say "Girls are here for me. I'm a player and I'm going to play the field."

I thought, *what a perfect comment for what we are about to talk about.*

I asked the boys to raise their hands if they felt they valued women. Only six boys had raised their hands.

"Why should I value women Coach?" One of the boys said. "All of the girls I know are bad. Most of them are hoes. They lie, steal, and cheat."

"Do we not do those same things?" I asked.

"Yeah, but, I mean its easy being a woman," the young man said. "The only hard thing about it is maybe having a baby. And that can't be that bad. Most of the girls I know have babies."

"Women are not just put on this Earth for our pleasure," I said. "There is a reason women give birth and we don't. It's hard, it hurts. Physically it's torture. I don't know that anyone would get born if it was up to men to give birth."

Everyone laughed.

"Maybe you're right," the young man said. "I know I don't want to get fat and get stretch marks."

TR TURNING BOYZ INTO MEN

Name

Date

What do you look for in a girl, what traits or characteristics?

What do you think a girl would say about you? Is it good, or bad? Explain

---

Once again I was amazed at the thought that went into their answers.

Most of the boys wanted love and friendship from a girl.

As what would become customary, Coach LaHue wanted to know how my meetings were going.

"How did it go today Ben?" Coach LaHue asked.

"Great," I said.

"What did you'll talk about today?" Coach LaHue said.

"Women, and what kind of things they looked for in a woman."

He laughed. "How did that go?" He said.

"Pretty good," I said.

"Did you get a lot of crazy answers, anything inappropriate?" He said.

"I got a couple of pretty silly answers," I said. "There were a few who said that they wanted a girl to have a nice butt, nice legs, that sort of thing. But all in all I thought it went pretty well."

"Good," Coach LaHue said. "You and Gene are doing a good job with that group."

"Thanks," I said. I started to walk out of his office when I paused, stopped, and looked at Neal.

"Coach LaHue," I said. "Would you be willing be to talk sometime with our group?"

"Sure Coach," he said. "I'd be more than glad to."

Chapter 23

GRAB LIFE

DODGE

High School Football Game of the Week

FOX SPORTS SOUTHWEST

Nov 6th, 7 P.M.

2008

We knew we were talented, and that this team had the makings of a playoff team. Most media outlets had predicted that we would make the playoffs and challenge Smithson Valley to win the District 26-5A crown.

Personally, I was excited that Coach LaHue decided to move me from wide receivers to coaching defensive backs. Most of my experience as a coach had centered around coaching the secondary. Once again I wanted to prove myself as a coach.

High expectations immediately turned into high stress and disappointment.

We were beaten badly 49-28 by Kerrville Tivy in our season opener.

Tivy had a good team, but we had beaten ourselves.

Defensively we played poorly, we didn't read our keys, and failed to play assignment football. The loss was compounded by the fact that it came at the hands of Kerrville Tivy. Coach LaHue had once been their head coach. He had resurrected their program and turned it into a winner. Additionally, Tivy's current head coach was his best friend, as well as his best man at his wedding.

We would have to wait a full year to get our revenge.

The following week we bounced back in spectacular fashion, thumping a good Converse Wagner team 31-7.

The win was very satisfying. We had suspended three defensive starters for the first half due to disciplinary reasons and played well without them. Among the suspended was our stud line backer, Keith Strong.

We opened district play with a 52-7 win over the Churchill Chargers. We whipped them in every phase of the game. It was a great win. We had executed our game plan to near perfection.

The Roosevelt Rough Riders would face the Lee Volunteers in the second week of district play. I've always found it challenging to try to hype up an opponent when they are simply not very good. If there is one team who is historically at the bottom of our district, it is Lee. We had a good week of practice and were supremely confident. But confidence turned to sheer terror as the Volunteers returned the opening kickoff ninety yards for a touchdown.

"Don't panic, we're all right," Coach LaHue said. "There is plenty of time left. Now let's go score."

We scored the game's next forty-two points and cruised to an easy 49-14 win.

My starting corner back, Spencer Davidson had been suspended for the first half for violating team rules.

At half-time I asked Coach LaHue what he wanted me to do in regards to Spencer.

"It's your call Coach," Coach LaHue said.

I wasn't quite sure how I wanted to approach the situation.

Midway through the third quarter, with the victory well in hand, Spencer asked if he could go in. He had asked numerous times during the course of the game, but his back up, Bruce Hendry, was playing well. I wanted to reward Bruce for his hard work in practice and somehow punish Spencer, hoping he would learn from his mistake.

"No," I said. "I'm going to hold you out. You'll start next week, so be ready."

I saw the tears roll down the side of his face. Under his breath, I heard him quietly say this is "bull shit."

It hurt me to see him cry, but his poor response had me convinced that I had made the right decision.

Our third district opponent was the Reagan Rattlers, who had gone 10-3 the previous year.

This week's game would have a playoff atmosphere. The game was a real bruiser. Both teams' defensive units played very well.

With the Rough Riders clinging to a 12-7 lead late in the fourth quarter, we were stopped on third down and would have to punt it back to the Rattlers.

Our punter, Spencer Davidson, who also our starting left corner, calmly jogged on to the field.

"Make sure of the catch first, and give us a good punt," I said.

Davidson smiled at me before he ran onto the field.

"Coach, I got you," he said.

Davidson hit a great punt, 43 yards with no return. The Rattlers would have to go a long way if they were going to win this game.

It was our night, on third down outside line backer Marquis Foster intercepted an errant pass. The game was over. We were 4-1, most importantly, 3-0 in District play.

I always marveled about how many small things go into a win that are never mentioned in the newspaper or noticed by the average fan. Defensively, everyone has to read their key and do their assignment. Offensively, it takes all 11 players executing, blocking, throwing, and catching to make a play work. On this particular night, I thought Davidson's punt was the play of the game.

The New Braunfels Unicorns would be our next victim, but it would not be easy. In another extremely hard fought-physical game, line backer Keith Strong played the game of his life.

He was all over the place. Early in the first quarter he had stripped the football from the Unicorns tailback and sprinted seventy yards for the touchdown. Late in the game he saved us again. New Braunfels was driving, only twenty-two yards from a game winning score. The Unicorns ran a screen, but Strong read it perfectly, intercepting the pass and nearly returning it for another score. We were victorious, surviving another 26-5A thriller, 12-7.

The San Antonio Johnson Jaguars presented us with a unique challenge. They were a brand new school, and their team was made up of mostly sophomore and juniors. Mentally, we were not prepared for the game.

The stadium's turf was brutally hot. It was wickedly humid. I thought, *great, leg cramps.*

We won 49-7, but played with less than stellar effort. If not for a last second Devin Haywood touchdown pass, the Rough Riders would have gone into the locker room deadlocked at seven to end the first half.

The Jaguars were well coached, and their kids played us hard. I clearly remember thinking as we shook hands with our opponents at the games conclusion, that had we been matched with a physically equal team, that we would have lost. I tried to erase the thought from my head, we had just won 49-7, but I was not very happy with our play.

The MacArthur Brahmas would be our next opponent. Offensively, we played very well. We won 38-28.

Our defense played well at times, but I felt like some weaknesses, schematically, had been exposed. Our inability to cover the flats in particular worried me. The flat is an area of the football field, that the outside line backer is responsible for dropping to in our defensive scheme. The flat is 10-12 yards deep.

In addition, two starters, brothers John and Joseph Phillips, had been injured, hospitalized, and lost for the season. Once again, I was unable to enjoy the victory. We were ranked #1 in the city, #1 in District 26-5A, and riding a seven game winning streak. We had locked up a playoff berth, regardless of how we fared our last two games. But I sensed danger, and I was right.

The Madison Mavericks had legitimate star power, led by future Texas A&M wide receiver Nate Askew. On any given down, but it happened often on third down, the Mavericks converted passes into our flats with ease. We would lose 35-21. We were 7-2, and still in first place.

The San Antonio Roosevelt Rough Riders versus the Smithson Valley Rangers November 6th matchup in many ways was very neat. For one, it was to be televised regionally by Fox Sports Southwest. Secondly, Craig Way, the voice of the Texas Longhorns would be doing the play by play commentary. Third, my friends and family could watch the game on television. I was thrilled and nervous at the same time.

The winner would capture the 26-5A championship.

We got the ball first and had a great opening drive. Our drive stalled inside the Rangers ten yard line. Our field goal attempt sailed wide right.

The Rangers responded with an eighty-seven yard time consuming drive.

Like our previous few games, on third and long the Rangers were able to convert, catching passes in the flat with ease.

Our offense had another great drive that once again ended with a missed field goal.

This night belonged to the Rangers, as they ultimately made more plays than we did.

We played hard, but not terribly well, we came up short 24-7.

Only two weeks after sitting atop the San Antonio high school football rankings, the Roosevelt Rough Riders found themselves in an uncomfortable position. Losers of two straight games and a regular season final record of 7-3, our confidence as a football team and coaching staff was shaken as we prepared for the playoffs.

We limped into the playoffs.

We were faced with the daunting task of playing Austin Westlake in the first round.

A good friend of mine, Steve Ramsey, (an old coaching buddy from when we were both assistants at Austin High) greeted me with a handshake and a hug. He was the offensive coordinator at Westlake, but his primary duty was to coach up the offensive line. Steve and I went way back together. We had both come to Austin High in 1999, and we had both left when Coach Moss had departed to Garland.

All week long I had tried to portray an aura of confidence, but I was very displeased with our defensive game plan, or lack of one. I knew what was going to happen.

Westlake ran almost the identical offense that we ran on our sub-varsity teams. And since I called our 9th grade B team's offense, I thought, *if we don't make some adjustment to what we do defensively, it could be a long night.*

It was. We were beaten convincingly, 42-21. I was not happy.

We had failed miserably to slow down Westlake's offense. I was angry and somewhat embarrassed. I could handle losing. But I felt like we had a poor game plan, and I was upset about it. I did not know what to do. How was I supposed to handle this new adversity?

I missed my family; I never saw Mandy or Isabella. I had almost convinced myself to resign. I was tired, and felt very burned out. I wanted to tell Coach LaHue how I truly felt. But at this point in time, I didn't feel good enough about our existing relationship. I did not want to tell him that I hated our defensive game plan that we had developed against Westlake. I didn't want to be a second guesser, *anybody can do that,* I thought. I did not want to seem disenfranchised or disloyal in anyway. At our next staff meeting I announced that I was considering leaving. I really thought this would please Coach LaHue, but it didn't.

He met with me privately a few days later and asked why I was thinking about leaving.

"Ben," Coach LaHue said. "You need to figure out what you really want to do. I'll give you some time to think about it."

One week later I slinked into Coach LaHue's office, with my tail between my legs.

"Coach," I said, full of shame and embarrassment. "I would still like to coach for you if you'll have me. I'm sorry for being such a pain in the butt."

Chapter 24

I was growing stronger as a man, but I still had days when I just wanted to throw my arms up and scream. I could not control all things. I could not manipulate life. I needed help.

I prayed to God.

Our Father, which art in heaven,

Hallowed be thy name.

Thy Kingdom come,

thy will be done,

In earth as it is in heaven

Give us this day our daily bread.

And forgive us our trespasses,

As we forgive them that trespass against us.

And lead us not into temptation,

But deliver us from evil.

For thine is the kingdom,

The power, and the glory,

for ever and ever.

Amen

I prayed every night. I was waiting for God to speak to me, I wanted to believe.

I decided that I would be at the mercy of the Lord.

Just weeks before I had planned to teach 'Making The New You' to my Boyz into Men group, I visited my mirror one more time. It was late and my wife was sleeping. I quietly closed the bathroom door and flipped on the light switch.

I stared at myself.

There I was, blinking.

My soul stared back and spoke to me.

If you're going to talk the talk, you have to walk the walk.

Although I was much older, many things from my childhood still haunted me.

I still harbored some resentment and feelings of hurt from when I was a child.

I still clung to those feelings. As a high school and college student I had used some of that anger to excel at school. I worked hard at school. I was a good student. But the A's and B's I made did little to fill the void that I felt.

I want some answers, I thought.

For as long as I could remember I had wanted answers. I had wanted them for a long time.

Why had my father not spoken to my mother in over twenty-five years?

I picked up my cell phone and called my father.

My step mother Brenda warmly answered the phone.

"Hi Ben," Brenda said. "How are you?"

"I'm doing okay, hanging in there," I said. "How are you?"

"Busy," she said. "Would you like to talk to your dad?"

"I would," I said. "I've got a couple of things I would like to ask him."

"Hold on one minute," she said. "He's outside."

"Oh, okay," I said, feeling a little relieved. I thought, *maybe I'll just call him another time.*

I could hear her open the door that led to the outside. "Ben is on the phone," she shouted in the direction of my father.

"He's coming," she said. "You know, he's very proud of you. He's been telling me about your group that you meet with."

"Is that right?" I said. I was grinning, feeling a little bit embarrassed. My body seemed to relax with the compliment.

"You certainly are an incredible coach, I love what you are doing for kids,I think it's great." She said. "Hold on, here's your dad."

"Hello," he said.

"Hi Dad," I said, taking a deep breath and slowly exhaling. "I'd like to talk, but it's not your usual talk about the (Texas) Longhorns or the (Dallas) Cowboys."

"Okay," he said. "What would you like to talk about?"

We talked for the next forty-five minutes; he answered just about all of my questions. By the time we had hung up I knew him in a way that I had not known him before. I better understood why he had no desire to see or to speak with my mother. He told me that he had often feared for my safety when I was allowed to see her as a child. He also shared with me that my mother had numerous affairs with other men while they were married. "After that weekend when you saw that stabbing (my uncle had attacked my aunt) in Corpus (Christi), that was it. I felt like you had been put into way too many unsafe . . . (he paused) . . . and some of the places that you stayed in . . . (he paused again) . . . I felt like I had to do something."

I had known my father for thirty-six years and learned more about him in less than one hour than I had ever dared to dream. We agreed to meet the following week and grab a hamburger together.

I was glad that I had called.

After hanging up I immediately thought of some more questions that I wanted to ask him.

Once again I retreated to my bathroom. I quietly brushed my teeth. Again, I found myself looking in the mirror.

I laid in my bed and stared at the ceiling. I couldn't sleep. I was still excited and thrilled that my father had been willing to talk to me. Not just talk, I thought, *he shared himself with me.*

He had gotten to the restaurant early. I was five minutes early, and he was already there. He was sitting down at a long rectangular table when I opened the heavy glass door that led into Chester's, a local hamburger dive. He stood up and looked at me. I saw his brown eyes flicker as I moved towards him. We greeted each other with a hug and a hand shake.

"So, what else would you like to know?" He said.

"Everything," I said. "How in the world did you ever meet my mother?"

"Oh boy, that's a tough one," he said. "I'll give it my best shot."

The very next day I called my mother.

"Mom, I need to see you," I said.

"That sounds fabulous," she said excitedly.

My mother and I had only seen each other a handful of times during my teenage years.

I was an adult now. I was married. I was a father.

She always tried to make every time that we did see each other special. She wanted to make up for lost time.

I understood that so I rarely objected. It was nice to see my mother from time to time. The last few times when I had seen her as a child or as a teenager were uncomfortable. We were forced to meet at a center where our visits were supervised as per court order. A Travis County court had found her unfit to be a parent.

I was on my way to meet her for dinner. I was running late. I hated to be late, I rarely was. I prided myself on being punctual.

The junior varsity baseball game I had just coached had run long. Somehow my team had managed to snatch defeat from the jaws of victory. I quickly showered and put on a fresh pair of clothes.

I was almost to the restaurant. Just a few more exits to go when I started to drift down memory lane. My thoughts betrayed me. I was there again . . .

The bar was smoky and reeked of stale liquor and beer. We were at the Hole in the Wall. The Hole in the Wall was my mother's favorite bar. She liked to go there to dance and see her friends. It often featured a band or an up and coming singer. Austin was the live music capital of the world. It was 1983. I was eight years old.

I pushed the door open and walked down the stairs. Grey billows of smoke followed me into the dark, almost pitch black room. Sharp-loud sounds penetrated the air. I was in the arcade section of the bar. I followed the glowing red sign.

.25

I inserted my quarter and off I went. Galaca was my favorite video game. I was good at it. I could last over an hour on just four quarters. It was getting late. I had run out of quarters. I found a relatively cozy spot on the ground to sleep . . . I awoke on the floor at my mother's apartment. I was tired, and I was cold.

The sound of a car's horn snapped me out of my daze.

This was my exit. Within seconds I was there.

I parked my green 2001 Toyota Camry towards the back of the parking lot. I didn't mind walking, but I did mind the sun. It was still damn hot.

As always, she greeted me with a big-wet red lipstick laden kiss. I was hungry and nervous. The two feelings combined to make my stomach very jumpy. We quickly ordered some food. We shared some chicken wings and a salad. I had informed her that I had several hard questions to ask her.

I stared at the Dr. Pepper that I had ordered to drink. Condensation had formed. My glass was sweating. I considered not asking what I had set out to do.

Finally, I was able to summon up the courage.

"Hey, Mom," I said. "I need to ask you a few questions. Please know I'm not trying to hurt your feelings or place judgment on you, but I have to know something."

"Okay Mijo (Mijo is the Spanish word for son)," she said.

"Why did you take me to bars and night clubs when I was a little boy?" I said.

There was a brief pause, it lasted about five seconds. My mother and I looked at each other. She studied my face, and then she began to cry. I attempted to comfort her by holding her hand.

"I'm so sorry, my son," she said, continuing to sob. "I just kind of wanted to have my cake and eat it too."

She continued crying. Her mascara smeared as she tried to dry her eyes.

"I was so young," she said. "You know, I couldn't really afford a baby sitter, and I had to work. When I was having fun, I wanted you near me." There was another pause.

"I'm sorry," she said. "I'm so sorry. I'm so ashamed."

"It's okay Mom, I'm not mad." I said.

"You know I love you, right son?" She said.

"Yes I do," I said. "I love you too."

The proverbial chip on my shoulder had fallen. Whatever pain, or feelings of neglect that I had held onto over the past several years seemed to vanish. I was happy. I smiled at her as I took another sip of my soda.

Chapter 25

"Why are we here?" I asked the players.

"To be a better man," the players shouted back.

"What?" I said.

"To be a better man," the players shouted louder.

"What is your job?" I asked.

"To love each other," the boys replied.

"I can't hear you," I said.

"To love each other," the boys roared back.

Today, we were going to attempt to tackle a very hard topic. Addressing one's hurt and shame.

I shared with the group my recent interactions I had with my Mom and Dad.

"Do you forgive your Mom?" one of the boys asked.

"Of course I do," I said. "I think forgiveness, when possible, is a big step in trying to be a man." He looked puzzled.

I shared with the boys one last final story from my childhood, one that I had kept filed away, buried under layers of hurtful memories.

I hated my childhood. Most of it I felt like I was in agony. I was lonely.

My father's second wife was a cold hearted person. She often would not feed me dinner and took deep pleasure in the fact that I was not allowed to see my mother. She knew how much I loved my mother and enjoyed hearing me cry myself to sleep. My father often worked late, so she would come into my room, just before bed to tell me something cruel. She almost always made sure that whatever she was going to tell me would hurt me and leave me unable to sleep.

"You are an evil and sneaky kid, and you're going to wind up crazy just like your mother."

I had very serious abandonment issues, and there was no way that I was going to tell my father about the things that she said to me on a regular basis. He was all that I had, and I was afraid that if I told him what was happening, and he didn't believe me, that I would lose him too.

I despised my stepmother. For seven years my life was miserable. But it did get better. My father got a divorce and remarried. This time to a much nicer woman.

I always wondered why Elaine hated me so much. I made good grades, I was quiet, I kept to myself, and I didn't want or need anything. Yet, she hated me.

Years later I got my answer, and I healed this particular wound.

One day after my high school graduation, I drove my 1982 Silver Honda Accord hatchback over to see Elaine. My car skidded to a halt as I attempted to park.

I sat in my car for about three minutes, I was ready. I found the courage to knock on the door where I had once lived. She answered and I asked if I could come in. It was the first and last time since my father's divorce that I saw her.

"Do you want anything to drink?" she said.

"No," I said. "I came here to ask you why you hated me so much."

She calmly looked me in the eyes and said, "I didn't hate you. I was just trying to hurt your father. I knew that it would hurt him if I was cruel to you."

I thanked her for her time and left. I actually felt good as I walked to my car. I felt strong.

"Man, I would have punched her in the face," one of the boys said. There were giggles in the classroom.

"Oh yeah," I said. "Well now it's time to work on you. Please fill out the handout and be prepared to discuss at the end if you feel comfortable doing so."

Making the "New You"

Name_____ Date_____

1. Have you been hurt? Are you scarred? If so, how? (please elaborate)

2. What do you do to protect yourself? (Do you have a defense mechanism?) If yes, please explain.

How do I get better? Will I get better? How do I heal? How do I make the new me?

- Accept the fact that you have been hurt, or that you are wounded
- Face (confront) your hurt

Chapter 26

Spring 2009

Coach Patrick Swoyer and I had just walked through the double doors that led to the boys' athletic facility. We knew instantly that something was terribly wrong. Crying students filled our hall way. There was a girl weeping heavily. Snot was visible in one of her nostrils.

"What's wrong?" I said as I tried to comfort her.

"He's dead," she said. "He's dead."

"Who, honey, who is dead?" I said.

"Keith, he's gone."

Within minutes it seemed as if the entire school was in mourning.

We (the coaching staff) had quickly learned that one of our football players, line backer Keith Strong had been killed in a high speed chase trying to evade the police. Apparently, he and some other adult aged men had been breaking into homes and burglarizing.

What a shame, I thought. *What a shame.*

Keith had been offered a full scholarship to play college football. He was only months away from graduation.

Fall 2009

Number 22 decals were placed on the back of our white helmets. Individual messages were proudly displayed on athletic tape by his team mates. With Keith fresh on our mind, we opened the 2009 season on the road, against Kerrville Tivy. It was loud, and very blue, Tivy's home colors.

We were ready for the Antlers.

A year earlier they had really embarrassed us, both the coaches and the players. This game had been circled on our schedule. We wanted a shot at redemption.

We played well, in all three phases of the game. Our offense, led by Brandon Armstrong and Devin Haywood kept Tivy on their heels all night. Defensively, we had come up with a plan to keep future Parade All-American quarterback Johnny Manziel in the pocket and under lots of duress.

Roosevelt went on to a 37-21 victory. The team gathered around Coach LaHue for post-game remarks. After the brief team talk, the players huddled and said, "That was for you Keith."

I prepped for my next job, passing out pizza and soda for the players. Smiles were abundant as we loaded the bus to go back to school.

On the bus ride back home we had learned that Converse Wagner, our next opponent, had upset Smithson Valley, the area's top ranked team. Wagner would come into next week's game as the #2 ranked team in San Antonio.

We hammered Wagner 31-16 on a wet and chilly Friday night. Both teams had to skip calisthenics as we waited for the heavy rain and lightning to subside.

Wagner could not stop our offense. Armstrong and Haywood had big nights to pace the Rough Riders. Our defense didn't play great, but we played hard and ran well to the football. Cornerback Crosby Adams would be caught peeking in the backfield and get burned for one of Wagner's two touchdowns. Little did I know that Crosby's lack of discipline and failure to play with proper technique would hurt us again the following week.

We opened district play with Churchill. A year ago we had destroyed Churchill 52-7, but that was a very different Charger team. This game would not be decided until the game's final play. It was a team we knew well, aside from playing against them every year; a familiar face was now at the helm for the Chargers. Coach Glenn Hightower was the new head coach at Churchill. I knew he would have them ready to play us. Having worked for him when I first came to Roosevelt, I felt like I knew what he was going to do. Coach Hightower is a very defensive minded coach, and I knew that he would play keep away from us. He believed in ball control, and since he knew that we had an explosive offense, he found a way to keep us off the field. His plan almost worked to perfection.

Controlling the clock and the flow of the game, Churchill looked poised to pull off the upset. Leading 14-10 late in the fourth quarter, things did not look good for the Rough Riders.

We mounted a great drive, but we came up short on third down. Coach LaHue burned his final timeout.

The crowd was going nuts, it was loud. *We believe, we believe,* was being chanted by the Roosevelt student body.

Facing a fourth and one from the Charger 14 yard line we were forced to go for it. The play was brought into the huddle, **'Rip Unbalanced 44 Bama Q.'**

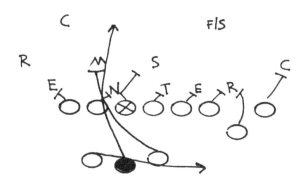

Churchill played it well; their player was sitting there waiting on the quarterback. Haywood looked like he would be stopped for a no gain. Somehow, he spun away from the tackler and raced into the end zone. Touchdown Rough Riders!

The Chargers still had some fight left in them. They mounted a drive to our thirty yard line, but facing a very long field goal, the Chargers elected to go for it. The Charger Hail Mary was deflected by cornerback Bruce Hendry and intercepted by our free safety Leland Young. We had dodged a bullet, winning 17-14.

Excited, but mostly relieved, I gave a big hug to running backs Coach Tate Demasco. Coach Demasco and I had not always been close; in fact our relationship had started negatively. But over the years we had developed a friendship. Mostly we shared the same feeling, we were glad to be 3-0.

We beat up Lee 49-20 the following week with it becoming more or less a glorified scrimmage. Defensively, we didn't play well, and I was deeply concerned. We were 4-0 and ranked #1 in the city, but just about everybody in District 26-5A can beat you. In my opinion, we had some very real weaknesses that a good offense would find and exploit. Unfortunately, I was right. We would lose our next two games, surrendering lots of points and yards.

The Johnson Jaguars, like the year before, had an excellent game plan for us. Ultimately, we lost a controversial 14-13 heart breaker to the Jaguars. It was our third consecutive loss. So much for being the top ranked team in San Antonio.

Some positives occurred during the course of the game: cornerback Crosby Adams had regained his confidence, and he would play great football for the remainder of the season. Most importantly, as a result of the way we lost the game, we became a team and rallied around each other.

While clinging to a 13-7 lead, free safety Leland Young fell on a Jaguar fumble with forty-nine seconds left. The game appeared over, but unexplainably, the ball was awarded to the Jaguars. The officials call was so bad that when we recovered the football, a Jaguar football player tossed his helmet about twenty yards after seeing the play. One of the Jaguar coaches tossed his head set when he saw the fumble. I watched him walk and pick it up after the ball was awarded to the Jaguars.

Two plays later, Johnson completed a thirty-four yard post to beat us. We had blown the coverage and lost the game. After the solemn bus ride back, I watched the games controversial play again and again on tape, as if expecting the call to be reversed. But you can't cry over spilled milk; we had work to do. It would take a near miracle for us to advance to the playoffs now. When you feel you have been cheated, you have to come back fighting, and we did just that, playing inspired football for the next three weeks.

We completely dismantled MacArthur; we probably played our best half offensively of the season. Our offense was firing on all cylinders, and it could not have come at a better time. We cruised to an easy 35-9 victory.

Nobody gave us a chance versus San Antonio Madison. Madison was ranked #2 in the State by many members of the associated press. They had several division one players on their team. They still had big play wide receiver Nate Askew (Texas A&M). In addition to Askew, Madison had two division one running backs in Aaron Green (Nebraska) and Troy Williams (UTSA). Green was an electrifying back, who could score anytime that he touched the ball. Earlier in the season he scored seven times and rushed for over 500 yards in a 63-56 win over Kerrville Tivy.

This particular night belonged to the Roosevelt Rough Riders. We dominated all game long, winning 31-14. It was special for me on several different levels, personally and professionally.

My daughter was on the sidelines performing with the Roosevelt cheerleaders. Leading 31-7 late in the third quarter, I got to sneak in a hug with Isabella as she was just a few feet behind our bench. My father and my stepmother were at the game, my brother in law Jesse was at the game with his son. Mandy and Ava, my youngest daughter, were all in attendance. I looked up to the stands to see all of my family having a blast, enjoying our win.

I thought, *at least for one evening, all seemed right in the Universe.*

I was able to savor the victory and see my family at the same time. It was a great night. In addition, I was very pleased with the corner backs. Crosby had basically shut down Nate Askew, their only real passing threat. By him doing that, it allowed us to load the box and focus on stopping the run.

Crosby played well and with a lot of confidence. Crosby also had a late interception and returned it to midfield.My other corner back, Bruce Hendry, played with great hustle. I thought the game was summed up best when Bruce sprinted forty yards across the field to give a crushing block to the Madison quarterback, leveling him and leaving him unable to finish the game during Crosby's return on an interception.

My guys, the entire team, played with incredible energy, and on this particular evening we could have beaten anybody.

"Win and you're in," was the mantra the Rough Rider corner backs said all week. Left for dead just three weeks earlier, Roosevelt would have to pull off the unthinkable in order to advance to the Texas high school playoffs. The Rough Riders would have to knock off the Smithson Valley Rangers, who had been to the playoffs thirteen consecutive seasons, a streak that dated back to 1995.

It was a great game, one that had four lead changes. The Rangers, to their credit answered every one of our scores through the games first three quarters. As my Rough Riders clinged to a 24-20 lead, the Rangers mounted a drive deep into our side of the field. With 1:46 remaining, cornerback Bruce Hendry intercepted an errant Smithson Valley pass at the Roosevelt 15 yard line.

I met Bruce with a high five and bear hug, and then I proceeded to tackle him. I was beyond happy for Bruce. He and Crosby had been much maligned during the 2009 campaign, and it was sweet to have his play seal the game's outcome. As we melted the game's final seconds away, I had to take a seat on our bench. With my hat drawn way down on my face, I sat and wept. I was overcome with emotion. Tears rolled down my cheeks as I soaked in the game's final moments. I know both Bruce and I felt vindicated.

Just a few days earlier at practice, Bruce was telling me that he was going to get an interception to win the game. Bruce could not catch a cold if his life depended on it; he had two hooves for hands. I told him that if we was right that I would take him out for dinner. The following week I happily made good on my promise. What a game. Both teams had given the 4,559 fans a very exciting evening of high school football.

Playoffs.

I think everybody on our staff felt that we would win our first round game. I remember thinking we were very quiet and flat in pregame, just kind of going through the motions. We had played at such a high level for the past three weeks.

We led Austin Bowie 28-18 going into the game's final quarter. It looked like we were going to win our first round playoff game.

Still leading by three with just under five minutes remaining, we called for a play action pass on a third and short. It was a great call. But somehow our wide receiver dropped the pass. He was too wide open.

We punted and our opponents drove the length of the field. They chewed up valuable time as we watched helplessly from the sideline as their tailback continued to punish us, breaking many arm tackles along the way. They scored a touchdown with less than a minute to go.

We had lost. It hurt.

All night long we tackled poorly. Bowie did all of its damage on the ground. They had abandoned their passing attack early in the first quarter when corner back Crosby Adams had intercepted an ill advised post and returned it fifty yards.

But it didn't matter now. Our season was over.

Chapter 27

Feb. 15th Items of discussion/agenda

—why are we here? To be a better MAN

—what is your job? To LOVE each other

*Coach Scoggins presentation about marriage

What it takes to make it work

*Coach LaHue talk

*David Robinson video on leadership

OUR FOUR RULES TO GUIDE US

1. He accepts responsibility

2. He leads courageously

3. He helps others

4. He does the right thing

"Why are you here?" I asked the players.

"To be a better man," the players shouted back.

"What?" I said.

"To be a better man," the players shouted louder.

"What is your job?" I asked.

"To love each other," the boys replied.

"I can't hear you," I said.

"To love each other," the boys roared back.

"Good morning boys," I said. "Please look at your notes that you have been given. Reference it when needed for today's lesson. I hope you enjoy this morning. I think you will."

The projector displayed Coach Gene Scoggins' power point presentation.

'Marriage is under attack'

Gene had designed an elaborate power point presentation. I could tell that he had spent hours on his lesson that he was teaching.

I was impressed. I listened closely, hoping that I would learn something. I had been a product of divorced parents, and I knew how it could impact children.

My phone vibrated, I was going to ignore it but then remembered I was expecting an important phone call. I walked out into the hallway so I wouldn't distract the kids from Gene's lesson.

"Hello," I said.

"Ben?"

"Yes," I said.

"It's Neal, I'm running about five minutes late," he said. "What room number are y'all in?

"Rough Rider 209," I said.

"See you in just a minute."

I walked back into our room. Gene was going over some startling statistics:

More than one out of every two marriages end up in divorce. Children of divorced parents are much more likely to commit suicide. Children of divorced parents are far more likely to be a bully. Children who are victims of abuse often abuse their own children. The statistics seemed to go on forever. It was a scary list.

Neal walked in just as Gene was wrapping up his presentation.

I thanked Gene for sharing and introduced our next speaker, but he didn't really need an introduction. We all knew him. The kids seemed amazed that he was there. Quiet whispers could be heard. "Hey, Coach LaHue is here."

"Thanks for allowing me to speak to you today," Coach LaHue said. "It's an honor. I'm sorry it's taken me so long to get up to one of these meeting. I've been wanting to and just haven't been able to find the time."

"Raise your hand if you don't have a father," Coach LaHue said. "Now raise your hands if your parents have gotten a divorce."

Twenty of the twenty-nine students had their hands raised.

Coach LaHue had his hand raised.

"I'm a product of divorce," he said. "I never really knew my father. I was raised by my mother. It was hard, man. But I turned to sports. My coaches and my team mates became my family. Football was my ticket out. It was a way for me to go to college."

The room was silent.

He continued sharing.

I learned things about Neal that I never knew. I suspected he had been hurt as a child, like I had. I thought, *he is human.* We had some common ground. Although he was probably not aware of it, I had a new level of respect for him. I appreciated him.

When Coach LaHue was done talking to the boys I thanked him for sharing.

"Coach, please remain standing." I said. "It is my pleasure to give you this."

I handed him a framed picture of Leland Young, Joshua Glass and Quenton Bradley signing their scholarship papers. Each of the three young men had signed it. Coach LaHue stood in the background of the picture.

"Coach, I know you kind of have a thankless job, and you deal with a lot of problems every day," I said. "But I want you to know how much we appreciate you." Applause erupted as he shook my hand and accepted his gift.

Later that day I popped into his office to talk to him.

"Coach," I said. "I wanted to say thank you."

"For what," he said.

"For keeping me around." I said.

"I also wanted to say that I am sorry. I'm sorry that it took me so long to buy into your system. But I think you can tell that I'm all in. I know we didn't get off to the best of starts, but I'm glad I'm here. Thank you."

There was a short pause, it lasted about three seconds.

"Ben, I hope you know I'm not worried about what happened when you first got here," Coach LaHue said. "If I was, I wouldn't have kept you around. Don't worry about it Bud. And thanks for the present, I appreciate it."

I started to walk out of his office, feeling satisfied with his answer. But I thought, *I'm not done. I have more to say.*

I popped my head back into his office, feeling sort of foolish as I smiled at him.

"Sorry Coach, one last thing I have to say," I said. "Last week you asked us at our staff meeting that if anyone is planning on leaving, to please let you know. Well, I'm one of the guys that you don't have to worry about. I'll definitely be back next year."

"Thanks Coach," Neal said. "That means a great deal to me."

Chapter 28

2010

What can I say about 2010, it was a great season. Exciting would definitely be one word that comes to mind. We had good people playing for us, and they were pretty darn good football players to boot.

2010 opened with a bang, and a great opponent. We opened our season with highly touted San Antonio Stevens. Stevens was picked to win their District and make a deep playoff run. They were also picked to dispose of my Rough Riders.

Well, the newspaper got two of their three predictions right.

Led by University of Texas bound Mykail Thompson, the Stevens Falcons drew first blood taking an early 7-0 lead. It would be one of their few highlights. Thompson and the Falcons were roughed up most of the evening. We scored the game's final 28 points and won by a score of 28-7. It was a good win. We had contained Thompson. Our quarterback Sean Alonzo had made it clear that he was our leader, playing with guts and courage. He had managed to play with a badly sprained ankle.

The win was costly to me and the Roosevelt secondary as two cornerbacks were injured in the games first quarter. One of them was lost for the season.

In pre-game I had visited with Stevens head coach Lee Bridges. Bridges had coached me when I was a senior at Austin High.

We chatted about the 1992 season, and the many journeys our coaching paths had taken us. We wished each other luck. But I think on this day luck had little to do with it. Our team was better prepared, and in better physical shape. The game's final score reflected it. Stevens would wind up having a terrific season, advancing to the State semi-finals.

Around San Antonio, Roosevelt had developed a reputation as being front runners. It was perceived that we played very well when things were going our way. But if bad things happened, and we fell behind to an opponent, that we would quit. It was also perceived and believed that we start fighting each other, and bickering with one another. I think we had that perception because we were an inner-city east side school.

A lot of teams fight and bicker when they lose. Football is an emotional game; it is not played by robots. In our case it was played by boys. Boys who have lots of wounds.

I hoped we would be able to prove to the city that we were not front runners, and that was a false misconception about Roosevelt. Our kids played hard, and with a lot of class.

The following week we played somewhat flat, but found a way to win. We defeated San Antonio Warren in overtime. Warren was a good defensive team, and would advance to the playoffs.

Unfortunately for the Rough Riders, week three matched us with the Judson Rockets, a perennial state power. The Rockets seem to have our number, physically and mentally. We scratched and clawed our way back into the game and trailed 24-17 with four minutes remaining, but a coverage bust on fourth down allowed the Rockets to run out the clock and ultimately beat us 31-17.

As we feared, and to the delight of our many detractors, some of our players pointed fingers and blamed each other for the loss on the bus ride back home. We had work to do, on and off the football field. Our defense had played poorly; we didn't stop the run or the pass. We would have to get better in order for us to make the playoffs.

Week Four.

We were scheduled to play the Round Rock Dragons at our home field, Heroes Stadium. Round Rock had just defeated a good Austin Bowie team, who had knocked us out of the playoffs just a year ago. But after watching three of Round Rock's game films, I just didn't think they could beat us. Our defense simply had superior personnel.

Round Rock did a lot of good things with formation variations and motion, but they just did not execute very well. That trend would continue for at least another week. Our defense dominated the Dragons all night. We defeated Round Rock 24-7.

September 24. Week 5, the opening of District 26-5A play. It was also my birthday. The secondary promised to make it a special day for me, and they delivered. We made easy work of the Lee Volunteers. By the time the first quarter ended, we led 21-0. We went onto to an easy 49-0 victory. "That one was for you Coach J," corner back Gerald Carson said.

We stunned top ranked MacArthur in overtime to win our second consecutive game in district play.

The Madison Mavericks loomed next.

2009 we had dominated them, easily winning 31-14.

This year's game would be different.

We led early, and went into halftime with the lead. But, it would not be our night. Down the stretch we failed to make stops and lost a hard fought game to the Mavericks.

As I feared, the finger pointing and excuse making immediately started on the defensive bus as we drove back to school. We were still not quite a team.

For the second consecutive year the Johnson Jaguars and Roosevelt Rough Riders traded blows and competed in an intensely hard fought game. This time we found a way to win it, despite having a controversial touchdown pass go in favor of the Jaguars.

Sean Alonzo led us on a last minute game tying score to force overtime.

In overtime, Alonzo and the Rough Riders would not be denied. It was our third victory in overtime. On what would be the game tying possession, Leland Young and I watched Sean Alonzo lead us down the field.

It was hard to watch, you could almost cut the tension filled air with a knife.

Facing several third and longs, it just didn't look like we were going to be able to find a way to force overtime.

Several back up players walked by Leland and I and said, "we're going to lose."

Leland immediately redirected them, "no we're not, Sean is going to lead us down the field. You have to have faith."

I was so proud of him. Leland had grown into an extraordinary young man. He was a leader, on and off the field. I smiled on the inside as Alonzo converted a third and long into a touchdown. Leland jogged onto the field to hold the PAT.

If we beat Churchill we would clinch a playoff spot with a game to go. Churchill had to win to get into the playoffs.

We played hard, but not especially well. With the game tied 14-14, it looked like we were going to play our fourth overtime game of the season.

On 3rd and 18 from midfield, Churchill threw a pass that looked like our strong side linebacker would intercept. Miraculously for Churchill, the ball was not only not intercepted, but deflected and popped up high into the air. It came down right in the arms of a Churchill wide receiver who caught the ball in full stride.

The wide receiver would not be dragged down until they were basically in field goal range. Churchill converted two more first downs and kicked a field goal to beat us. It was a deflating 17-14 emotional loss. We would have to beat a good Reagan Rattler football team to advance to the playoffs.

The Rattlers were led by star quarterback Trevor Knight. Knight was a four star recruit, and had verbally committed to play college football at the University of Oklahoma.

Just a year earlier Knight and the Rattlers had scorched our defense for thirty-nine points and started us on our three game losing skid. We wanted a chance at redemption.

Coach Griffin and I challenged the secondary all week in practice; we basically told them that if we played well as a unit, we would win. They were going to throw the ball, and test us.

I knew they were going to go throw early and often at our corners.

Versus Madison we had failed to stop the hitch, the out, and the comeback. The out is a five step passing play in which the wide receiver runs 10-12 yards, sticks his foot in the ground, and runs out to the sideline.

We had played too soft, and although I taught them that we had underneath flat help from our outside linebackers, it was very apparent after watching 9 games that they were not going to get any help. I tightened them up and slowed their back pedal down. We altered our stance and worked harder on our three step reads.

We were ready!

We intercepted three passes, and caused four turnovers. We completely dismantled the Rattlers, clinching a spot in the Texas State playoffs.

We led 24-3 at the half, and it was fun to see all of our hard work in practice pay off. On the sidelines it was the Rattlers who were bickering and fighting, we would play another week. I thought, *front runners my ass!*

When the playoff pairings were announced, I think our kids were disappointed and mentally somewhat psyched out. Depending on how you viewed it, it was our fortune, or misfortune, to be paired with Cibolo Steele.

As a coach, I felt that Steele had a good chance to win the state championship. They were loaded with talent, with several players committed to play Division One college football. Led by the nation's most highly coveted and recruited running back Malcolm Brown, Steele was a formidable opponent. Brown was a Parade All-American, and the pride of the Texas Longhorns recruiting class.

We had already beaten one Texas commitment, as we demolished MyKail Thompson and the Stevens Falcons 28-7 in week 1 of the season. But we had not really faced anyone like Brown. He was powerful, fast, and tough. The newspaper and many national magazines compared him to Earl Campbell and Cedric Benson. It was a good comparison.

First quarter.

After a Roosevelt punt, we hammered Brown and the Steele Knights.

On third down we stuffed Brown and the Knights. Leland Young made a fantastic open field tackle on

Brown. But at the end of the play, somebody had rolled up on Leland and hit him from behind. Leland Young limped off the field.

We were told that he might have a broken leg. With Leland out of the game, our defensive fits were simply not the same.

Second quarter.

The Knights devastated us with a relentless rushing attack. Brown had an eye popping 95 yard touchdown run in which he seemed to make us look like rag dolls.

Rest of the night.

They continued to pound us on the ground.

Trailing 21-7 in the third quarter, Leland tapped me on my shoulder. I took off my head set and looked at him.

"What," I asked.

"Coach," Leland said. "I can play."

"Let me see you sprint," I said.

Leland attempted to run just behind our bench. He was clearly hurting. One of his legs seemed to drag behind the rest of his body. I checked with the team doctor. He said it was my call. He was cleared to play.

I made Leland practice a few more sprints on the sideline. He was slowed and clearly not able to play effectively. He could not cut or change direction. I had the doctor examine him once more. Leland winced in pain when the doctor touched his leg.

I gave Leland a big hug as he sat on the team doctor's examining table. I looked into the bleachers, trying to catch a glimpse of his parents. I could not see them.

"I love you Leland, and I'm proud of you," I said. "But I can't put you in this game." I paused.

"If you were my son I wouldn't want you to play," I said. "You're injured, my man. It's just bad luck."

"I understand," Leland said. He looked down at the ground, slapping the air in frustration.

He became a cheer leader and tried to help our back up free safety understand his fits and alignment. But it was too late.

We were not the same defense without Leland Young.

Brown and the Knights defeated us 33-13. Steele was not to be stopped. They dismantled all of their opponents, winning the 2010 5A State Championship.

Chapter 29

August 8, 2011

The Roosevelt Roughriders came together for its first practice at seven in the morning. It was already hot. The sky was slightly over cast as the coaches set up their drills for the morning workout.

"What's up Coach Jacobs?" asked Brit Navarro. Brit was one of my defensive backs, we had grown close and talked often. He gave me a cool hand shake and a slight hug.

"Coach J," said another of the defensive backs, giving me a playful push. "What's going on, you ready to do this?"

I looked around as the rest of the football players jogged their way out of the locker room and onto the practice field.

Momentarily I stared at the apartment complex across the street from our practice complex.

I quickly refocused and watched as some of the boys greeted their individual position coaches.

A small line of young men had assembled, they were waiting for me. I didn't want to keep them waiting.

They patiently waited, one after another as I took turns giving out hugs.

"Coach, it's good to see you," defensive back Seven Ellis said. "I missed you. I love you."

I thought, *Football season. It was good to be back.*

Chapter 30

August 25, 2011

Our first *Making Men* class was getting ready to begin.

Music from my Sprint LG cell phone filled the team room.

It was eight o'clock on a warm Thursday morning. Sixty-five football players sat in their chairs, armed with spirals and pencils. Their eyes studied me. They were ready to learn.

"Why are you here?" I asked the players.

"To be a better man," the players shouted back.

"What?" I said.

"To be a better man," the players shouted louder.

I was there for the same reason.

BEN JACOBS was born in Austin, Texas, in 1974.

THE AUSTIN YEARS

Austin High School

1999	Defensive Backs	3-7
2000	Defensive Backs	8-3
2001	Defensive Backs	8-3

Reagan High School

2002	Defensive Coordinator	10-3
2003	Defensive Coordinator	6-5

Travis High School

2004	Special Teams Coordinator	7-4

THE SAN ANTONIO YEARS

Roosevelt High School

2005	Defensive Backs	4-6
2007	Wide Receivers	5-5
2008	Defensive Backs	7-4
2009	Defensive Backs	7-4
2010	Defensive Backs	7-4
Won/Loss		72-48
The game of life		???

Bibliography

Marx, J. (2003) *Season of Life.*
New York. Simon and Schuster.

Section 8. Retrieved July 14, 2011, from www.
affordablehousingonline.com/section8housing.asp

The Lords Prayer. Retrieved July 16, 2011, from www.
lords-prayer-words.com/lord_traditional_king_james.
html